# WHY THE
# HOLOCAUST

*Destination Israel*

## BY NOAM COHEN

*ISBN: 9798882764547*

*Printed in the USA*

*Cover Design: Chris Maita*
*Editing: Teresa Sarros*
*Publishing: Cherri Beard*

*For more information about the author,*
*Visit: www.declaringzioninternational.org*
*e-mail: declaringzionintl@yahoo.com*
*YouTube: Declaring Zion International*
*Facebook: Deborah N Noam Cohen*

*I am forever grateful to my beloved wife, Deborah, for her help, support and encouragement in writing this book. She was the one who showed me the ancient path which led me to the Messiah, Yeshua, my Redeemer. You are the best gift God has ever given me.*

# Table of Contents

# Preface

As a child born in Israel, I remember observing Holocaust Memorial Day every year. This is a very special and somber day set aside to remember the events of the Holocaust. I will always remember those days from my childhood, as they affected me so much.

I used to ask my parents, "Where was God?" and, "Why did God allow it to happen?" But the answer I got was not enough then and it is not enough now. But we will explore that later.

I realize now that even as a youth I searched for truth, for the meaning of life, and for the Way of life that would improve me and make me stronger physically, emotionally, and mentally. This search intensified as I grew up, especially after my time in the Israeli army, and led to my going to Japan.

At the age of twenty-three I left Israel for Japan because I thought martial arts was the way of life that I was seeking. And in order to live it fully, I believed it was best to go to where it all began, to Japan, to learn the art of the Ninja.

In the twenty-one years that I lived in Japan, I learned a lot about life, and I realize now that one of the main things that pushed me to want to learn the secrets of life was the Holocaust.

If one does not have a deep understanding of life, then he will not understand death, and that is what the Holocaust is all about. After I came to believe in Yeshua upon returning to Israel, I found that the Bible says in

1

Romans 14:8, "For if we live, we live to the Lord; and if we die, we die to the Lord."

In this book, I will share the insights which the Holy Spirit has given me regarding the Holocaust, and my hope is that it will give you insights about your own life as well.

There is no doubt and no need to argue the fact that the Holocaust was the most devastating, sickening event in human history. But what I am trying to do through this book is open people's eyes to see beyond the pain, the horror, and the sorrow of it and focus on His will in it.

I started writing this book on August 22, 2012. It has been over ten years and the Lord has taken me on quite a journey. I have learned much through this effort, and I am sure I will learn much more as the journey continues.

I have tried to be as objective as possible on this subject through my eyes as a Messianic Jew.

God bless,

Noam Cohen

# Introduction

I had always prided myself in being a liberal man, worldly minded, letting people believe in whatever they wanted to without argument. But since coming to faith in Yeshua (Jesus), I can no longer be quiet. My heart in writing this book is to reach secular Jews who don't follow God at all, religious Jews who feel trapped in their traditions, and Christians who are sincerely wanting to understand the Jewish roots of their faith.

The Holocaust has meaning for all these groups, and through this book, I will explore what I believe God wants to teach us about this event and how it affects all of us.

In this book, I am using scriptures from the New Testament as well as the Old Testament. It should not stop Jews from reading this book since the New Testament was written by Jews, and the fact that many Jews rejected Yeshua (Jesus) at that time is not a reason to be alarmed or worried since most Jews also rejected the prophets of the Old Testament in their day.

Another issue regarding Yeshua is related to the destruction of the temple. Here is a question we can all ask ourselves: Do we believe that the Lord, the God of Abraham, Isaac, and Jacob, would just abandon His people and not give them hope or warning before the destruction of the second temple? Before the destruction of the first temple, God warned Israel through the prophets and gave them hope that in seventy years they would return home.

So also, before the destruction of the second temple, God sent Yeshua to warn Israel and to show His people the new way to Himself without the Holy Temple, knowing that this would help them spiritually in exile, too. That is why Yeshua was focused on the Jews and not on the Gentiles at that time. He told His disciples in Matthew 10:5-6, "Do not go into the way of the Gentiles, and do not enter a city of the Samaritans. But go rather to the lost sheep of the house of Israel."

It would be beneficial for us to use the New Testament to understand the spiritual walk the Jews could have had, before and during the Holocaust, if they had accepted Yeshua.

But the warnings are also for the Christians. Several years ago, my beloved wife and I were in the United States, and I was preparing to speak to a men's group at a church. The Holy Spirit told me that I wasn't seeing the whole picture regarding the Holocaust because I wasn't thinking about how it affects Christians. I was shocked because I had always believed the Holocaust was an event that was specifically for my people, the Jews. The Holy Spirit drew me to Romans 11:21 that says, "For if God did not spare the natural branches, He may not spare you (the wild branches) either." Wow. He was talking to the non-Jews!

I felt like the Lord was relating it to the Holocaust. That since the Jews were not spared from their Holocaust, He may not spare the Christians from their own Holocaust.

I know that's a bold statement. But it is not important to me whether you agree or disagree with what is written in this book, but that you learn and gain new insights from it and not just accept at face value what happened in the Holocaust.

As Jews, the Holocaust taught us that we must have our own country and an army to protect us, and that we cannot rely on other nations to prevent us from experiencing another Holocaust.

BUT WHAT DID WE LEARN SPIRITUALLY FROM THE HOLOCAUST? That is the greater question. And I am attempting to find the answer to it in this book.

# Faith, Death, and Destiny - Israel

Since I am going to look for the spiritual meaning or reason for the Holocaust, it is important to clarify some spiritual issues, starting with the meaning of faith.

The word "faith" in English does not give us any idea, in and of itself, what the word means. The Hebrew language is visual and symbolic and gives us a deeper meaning of words. Let me give you an example.

"Emuna" is the Hebrew word for "faith." The root of the word is "emun" which means "trust" and the last letter in the word is "Hay" which represents God. So in Hebrew, the word means "trust God." "Hay" is the letter that the Lord added to Abram's name, and he became Abraham. And the same for his wife Sarai, who became Sarah. Names in Hebrew have very specific meanings and define the person by describing their character or purpose. The addition of the letter "Hay" meant that Abraham and Sarah were now walking with God and had essentially been commissioned into the purpose God had called them to. God had inserted Himself into their lives!

"Amen" is also a root of the word "trust" in Hebrew, "emun." And what do we say at the end of a prayer? "Amen." This shows that a core ingredient of faith is acceptance - of His way, His timing, His direction, and His will. It sounds simple and easy, but our logical minds don't always see it that way, especially when things are not going the way we think they should.

For example, it is easier for us to accept the death of a ninety-year-old man than the death of a twelve-year-old boy. That is when we really struggle with our faith and cry out, "Why, Lord?" It is a hurdle for our faith to overcome. I will try to examine how we deal with such hurdles.

King David is an inspirational figure whose walk of faith we can all learn from. When his son was sick, he pleaded with God for the child (2 Samuel 12:22-23). He fasted and laid on the ground for seven days. But then when the child died, he got up from the ground, bathed, changed his clothes, and asked for food. He said, "While the child was alive, I fasted and wept; for I said, 'Who can tell whether the Lord will be gracious to me, that the child may live?' But now he is dead; why should I fast? Can I bring him back again? I shall go to him, but he shall not return to me."

King David went on living without any anger toward God for not letting the child live, nor did he indulge in self-pity. He was at peace.

Further thoughts about death are required since the Holocaust is about death, so we need to have clarity regarding the spiritual aspect of death. It is a subject that is not spoken about enough in churches. Like if we don't talk about it, then we don't have to deal with it.

I was asked to speak at a funeral, and during the service I said that the church does not prepare us for the death of a loved one. Just as we cannot stop the rain, death is inevitable. And just as we can take an umbrella so we will not be drenched by the rain, so also faith helps us not to be overwhelmed by death. That umbrella is our shield of faith, as mentioned in Ephesians 6:16 where it says, "…above all, taking the shield of faith with which you will be able to quench all the fiery darts of the wicked one."

I would like to examine the issue of death from the Word of God, as it is essential to our walk of faith. 2 Corinthians 1:9 clearly states, "Yes, we had the sentence of death in ourselves, that we should not trust in ourselves but in God who raises the dead..." Death humbles us and helps us to trust Him.

But when we ignore the subject of death, we become increasingly self-focused and learn to trust in ourselves more and more and in God less and less. We know in our minds that one day we will die, but we suppress that knowledge and end up living like we will never have to face it. We unconsciously behave as though we are immortal.

It usually isn't until we are faced with the death of a loved one that we realize our immortality, and we are devastated by it. But the fact is that no one can guarantee we will live another day. Only the Lord knows the number of our days.

The Coronavirus in 2020 caused the whole world to be more aware of death, and that is why it unbalanced most of us, believers and non-believers alike.

We need to live each day knowing it could be our last. James 4:13-14 describes it well. "Come now, you who say, 'Today or tomorrow we will go to such and such a city, spend a year there, buy and sell, and make a profit;' whereas you do not know what will happen tomorrow." Therefore, verse 15 tells us how we should think, and that we should say, "...If the Lord wills, we shall live and do this or that."

Ecclesiastes 9:5 says, "For the living know that they will die; But the dead know nothing..." This is where believers have the advantage over non-believers. Believers are not unbalanced by death. Revelation 12:11 tells us that we overcome the enemy by the blood of the Lamb and by the word of our testimony, and we do not love our lives to the death. Meaning that believers are detached from their death and know it is only an event that will take them to be with the Lord.

To understand the spiritual meaning of death, we need to go to the very beginning. The Lord told Adam that if he ate from the tree of the knowledge of good and evil, he would die. But he didn't die. Did the Lord lie to him or tell him that just to scare him? Of course not! That is not how the Lord is; that is how we are. When we want someone not to do something, we threaten him or her. God loves us and wants to protect us.

The Bible shows us what death is – a change of reality. Genesis 3:16-19 describes the new reality after death (sin) entered the world. For Adam and Eve (and their descendants), it meant working hard for food, experiencing painful childbirth, etc. A new world with new physical sensations they hadn't experienced in the Garden of Eden.

As we learned, faith is about trusting God. We know that trusting anyone takes time, and so it is with the Lord. Knowing and understanding another person is crucial. Trusting God, an entity that we cannot see, requires that and more, especially if we are to live by faith. "For we walk by faith, not by sight." (2 Corinthians 5:7). "So then faith comes by hearing, and hearing by the word of God." (Romans 10:17).

Therefore, hearing the Lord is crucial to our walk of faith, just as hearing the other person is important in developing any relationship. If we do not focus first on hearing Him, but instead on doing for the Lord, as the Israelites said in Exodus 24:7, "…All that the Lord has said we will do, and be obedient (hear)," then there is bound to be miscommunication that comes from not hearing God and results in focusing on ourselves and our doing.

For example, when I lived it Japan, I was very self-focused in my search for the way of life of the warrior. God was not in my life. It was all about my self-development. When I met the woman, who is now my wife, for the first time in Qumran, I asked her, "How come you know my God and I don't?" She said it was because I never looked for Him. That was so true.

We tend to live by sight and not by hearing because we have more security in our sense of well-being that has been developed through experiences and habits where sight is used more than hearing.

"Seeing is believing" is a common saying today. It was even more common in the days of the Bible. In John 20:25, Thomas said, "…Unless I see in His hands the print of the nails, and put my finger into the print of the nails, and put my hand into His side, I will not believe."

Even today, many rely on a physical representation of the cross for security as Christians by wearing the symbol of the cross. There is nothing wrong with wearing it, but it can be false security to the one who does not understand the power of the work of the cross and who has not really given his life to Yeshua.

We also tend to listen to people rather than to God. The religious Jews are focused on hearing from the rabbi, not from God. And it is through their doing and not doing that they hope God sees them and knows their faith. But our faith should not be based on men's wisdom but in the power of God (1 Corinthians 2:5). If we focus on our leaders instead of the Lord, then our faith is shaky.

Even today, many Jews believe that their good deeds are enough for the Lord. But as it was not enough for the Jews in Europe during the Holocaust, so it is not enough now, nor will it be in the future. Good deeds do not help you to know God and His will. "For by grace you have been saved through faith, and that not of yourselves; it is the gift of God, not of works, lest anyone should boast." (Ephesians 2:8).

The Lord wants us to listen to Him. We see throughout the Bible what happens when we do not hear the Lord. Zechariah 7:13 says, "'Therefore it happened, that just as He (the Lord) proclaimed (called) and they (the people of Israel) would not hear, so they called out and I would not listen,' says the Lord of hosts."

The English word "obey" that is used often in the Bible actually means "hear His voice" in the Hebrew. In Deuteronomy 28:1, our English Bible says, "Now it shall come to pass, if you diligently obey the voice of the Lord your God..." In Hebrew, it says, "hear and obey."

In the English translation you fail to see the emphasis on hearing. The word "hear" in Hebrew that is used here is "shema." The first two letters (pronounced "Shem") means "Name" ("The" Name, "The" Lord). Interesting coincidence! The last letter, "Ayin," means "eye" or "to see." Therefore, you can say that if you HEAR the Lord, you will SEE the Lord!

Revelation 3:20 really demonstrates the connection between hearing Him and seeing Him. "Behold, I stand at the door and knock. If anyone hears My voice and opens the door, I will come in to him and dine with him, and he with Me." Only if we hear Him will we then see Him and have relationship with Him.

The Shema is the most famous calling to the people of Israel. Deuteronomy 6:4 says, "Hear, O Israel: The Lord our God, the Lord is one!" It is the central theme of the Jewish religion and is said at the time of death, on the Day of Atonement, and in daily life in what we call "Kiriat Shema" every morning and evening.

In Mark 12:29, Yeshua also said that the first commandment is "Hear, O Israel, the Lord our God, the Lord is one." In both cases, the emphasis is on calling the people to hear.

In the book of Jeremiah, you see again and again the results of not hearing the Lord. One example is in Jeremiah 6:19. "Behold, I will certainly bring calamity on this people – the fruit of their thoughts, because they have not heeded my Words nor My law, but rejected it."

We see again clearly that hearing is crucial to knowing Him and creating a relationship of trust. Unfortunately, most of us follow our own hearts rather than the Lord's way, as it says in Jeremiah 16:12, "… each one follows the dictates of his own evil heart, so that no one listens to Me." And the result of that is in the next verse, "Therefore I will cast you out of this land into a land that you do not know, neither you nor your fathers; and there you shall serve other gods day and night, and I will not show you favor."

In Jeremiah 35:17, we get an idea of the consequences of not hearing the Lord and why any calamity would come upon Israel. "Therefore thus says the Lord God of hosts, the God of Israel: 'Behold, I will bring on Judah and on all the inhabitants of Jerusalem all the doom that I have pronounced against them; because I have spoken to them but they have not heard, and I have called to them, but they have not answered.'"

There is another thing that hinders our hearing Him, and that is the issue of our sins. "But your iniquities have separated you from your God; and your sins have hidden His face from you, so that He will not hear." (Isaiah 59:2).

After the destruction of the second temple, the Jews no longer had a way to redeem them from their sins, because it was impossible to perform the temple sacrifices. This resulted in being separated from God. Only belief in Yeshua's sacrifice can bridge that separation. That is why Yeshua came before the destruction of the second temple, to be the bridge to God.

I can be a witness to how important it is to hear the Lord. In the first week of February, 2020, when the Coronavirus had broken out in China but had not yet spread to the world, I was awakened around 3:00am and I went to my study to pray. My spirit was very agitated, and I cried out to the Lord, asking Him to show me what was wrong. When I prayed and asked the Lord for understanding, the Holy Spirit told me that a change was coming that would affect my employment and my location. Then I saw a vision of the northern part of Israel, and I realized that we needed to move to the north. The next morning, I told my beloved wife, and in June we moved from Jerusalem to a house by the Sea of Galilee.

That move helped us to go through the Coronavirus period with much more peace and comfort. I didn't know that huge changes were coming to the whole world. I thought it was just something personal for us. But that's how God works. It changed our lives and spared us from being locked down in a crowded city. I am so thankful that He spoke and I heard and obeyed His voice.

To trust Him, we need to know Him. "In all your ways acknowledge (know) Him and He shall direct your paths." (Proverbs 3:6). After all, how can you trust someone you don't know?

Knowing Him is not an easy task, and just using our sharp minds is not enough. 1 Corinthians 1:21 says, "...the world through wisdom did not know God..." and, again, that is why our faith "...should not be in the wisdom of men but in the power of God." (1 Corinthians 2:5).

In Hosea 6:6, we see how much the Lord wants us to know Him. "For I desire mercy and not sacrifice, and the knowledge of God more than burnt offerings." It shows that the people of Israel were content to just make sacrifices and give offerings to the Lord. It made them feel spiritually secure, and they could go on with their daily lives, having peace with the Lord without really knowing Him. Do we see a similarity now?

Many people just go to church on Sunday, give tithes, and are at peace spiritually for the rest of the week. This can result in considering themselves to be Christians, but due to worldly influences, end up not behaving as Christians the rest of the week. Romans 7:25 says, "... with the mind I myself serve the law of God, but with the flesh the law of sin." We can easily deceive ourselves.

Not knowing Him can also result in not understanding what is happening in our lives when hard times come.

Look at the simple faith of Job who asked in Job 2:10, "Shall we indeed accept good from God, and shall we not accept adversity?" If we can have that kind of simple faith, then we can have the peace of God by accepting the hard times that come and by trusting in Him.

Job knew what he was talking about. He actually experienced something of a personal holocaust – he lost everything and all his family except for his wife. Yet his reaction was that of a true believer: "The Lord gave, and the Lord has taken away; Blessed be the name of the Lord." (Job 1:21). How simple and yet not easy to do.

That brings us to another issue of our faith, and that is "simplicity." 2 Corinthians 11:3 warns, "But I fear, lest somehow, as the serpent deceived Eve by his craftiness, so your minds may be corrupted (and led away) from the simplicity that is in Christ."

We complicate things because of our reasoning minds. I really learned this when I studied martial arts in Japan. There, people are taught to "feel and act" more, and to "think" less.

When we have faith in His word, it brings more stability, clarity, and focus to our walk. Paul said to the Colossians that he was "...rejoicing to see your good order and the steadfastness of your faith in Christ." (Colossians 2:5).

Another issue that affects our walk of faith is who we follow. I spoke earlier about how a lot of Jews today only do what their rabbi says. We see from the Old Testament that the people of Israel wanted to follow a leader and not God. "And the Lord said to Samuel, 'Heed the voice of the people in all that they say to you; for they have not rejected you, but they have rejected Me, that I should not reign over them.'" (1 Samuel 8:7).

That is because they wanted to be like all the other nations. It was more convenient and easier to follow a human being who would lead them to war and handle their spiritual issues, just like it is easier to obey the rabbis today in all that they decide regarding your affairs than it is to follow the Lord.

We see the same problem in the church, where people only follow the pastor instead of relying on their individual walk with the Lord in a personal relationship.

Putting our trust in men and not in God directly has never been what the Lord wants for us. Our security should be in God and not in a human leader or government. Jeremiah 17:7-8 says, "Blessed is the man who trusts in the Lord, and whose hope (security) is the Lord. For he shall be like a tree planted by the waters, which spreads out its roots by the river..." But "Cursed is the man who trusts in man and makes flesh his strength..." (Jeremiah 17:5).

When we are focused on trusting men, we fail to see God's work in our lives, and that can lead to disaster. Isaiah 5:12-13 says, "But they do not regard the work of the Lord, nor consider the operation of His hands. Therefore my people have gone into captivity, because they have no knowledge..."

This is the same as the Jews in Europe who went into the Holocaust without knowing why.

In Hebrews 11:1, you see the definition of faith. "Now faith is the substance (assurance) of things hoped for, the evidence (proof) of things not seen." Hebrews 11:6 tells us why faith is important, "But without faith it is impossible to please Him (God), for he who comes to God must believe that He is (exists) and that He is a rewarder of those who diligently seek Him."

Yeshua is the only way to the Father. "Therefore, having been justified by faith, we have peace with God through our Lord Jesus Christ (Yeshua the Messiah)..." (Romans 5:1).

If we follow Yeshua, He will lead us to the Father. But for us to follow Yeshua, we need to deny ourselves. Matthew 16:24 says, "If anyone desires to come after Me, let him deny himself, and take up his cross, and follow Me."

Denying ourselves needs to be reflected in our daily life, in how we handle the world. It is not only a state of mind. Denying yourself seems abstract, but it means to not put yourself, your feelings, ideas, moods and issues first, but to put the Lord first. It sounds easy, but it is not. Most of us, myself included, have to be completely broken in order to get to this point. One of the benefits of getting to that point of denying yourself is to be able to be detached from the world and from yourself.

Aren't most of us distracted with the issues of the world? We may not think we are, but a crisis – for example, the Coronavirus – can bring it to the surface. When our normal routine is disrupted, it becomes obvious how distracted we can become.

1 Corinthians 7:29-35 tells us how to live in the world and not be of the world, and the goal is in verse 35, "And this I say for your own profit, not that I may put a leash on you, but for what is proper, and that you may serve the Lord without distraction."

We need to show the Lord in actions, not only in words, how much we are willing to sacrifice of ourselves for Him. Yeshua clarified that when He said that if we wish to follow Him, then we need to deny ourselves. What we really need to sacrifice nowadays is not a lamb, but ourselves, as I mentioned earlier. "For if we live, we live to the Lord; and if we die, we die to the Lord." (Romans 14:8).

Another reason why it is important for us to deny ourselves is stated in Psalm 46:10 where it says, "Let go and know that I am God." You probably have always heard it as, "Be still, and know that I am God;" That is the difference between the Hebrew and the English translation. The Hebrew gives a deeper meaning. We need to let go of the tight grip of control we have on our lives and let Him take over for us to really come to know Him. It doesn't mean for us to completely let go, but to loosen our grip, hold on lightly, allowing Him to mold and direct our lives. Only when we deny ourselves can we let go of the control we try to hang onto through our thoughts and feelings.

Faith is letting go of our control on our lives. We can do this by casting our burden on Him, as Psalm 55:22 says, "Cast your burden on the Lord, and He shall sustain you;" We realize that He truly is the only one who can sustain us. We cannot do it in our own strength.

Again, not an easy task, as we have our way of doing things and handling problems. That is why, in most cases, we need to be broken in order to untie us from our insistence on doing things our own way.

As a simple exercise to show you how hard it is to let go of this control and how hard it is to live by faith and not by sight, I recommend you try to walk in a secure open path with your eyes closed. You will soon find out that even though the area is clear, and logically you should not worry, you will not be able to keep your eyes closed for more than a few feet. That is the power of the attachment you have to doing things by habit. You are not used to walking with your eyes closed, even in a safe area.

The Jews in exile for centuries had believed that Israel was the Holy Land, yet it was not connected to their walk of faith. They didn't make it a priority to move there. The Jews would have continued living in exile if it were not for the Holocaust and the persecution in Russia that caused many to move to Israel. It is sad to say that without the Holocaust, Israel would not have been established.

This is not to say that Christians are perfect. I believe that most believers, myself included, go through times of speaking and acting as though they have no faith at all, just as the disciples behaved when facing the storm in the boat, even when Yeshua was with them. What we need to do, though, is be aware of our temporary lack of faith, repent, and try to learn from it. We don't need to obsess about it because that can cause us to focus too much on ourselves and away from the Spirit.

You can clearly see how Yeshua is essential for our walk of faith, but many Jews have rejected Him. One reason for it is that it requires humility. This is so contradictory to their basic prideful nature, which I believe comes from

Jacob. Jacob would not let go of the angel. Neither could I before I got saved, so I can truly attest to that.

Since Israel came from the sons of Jacob, it is important to understand Jacob's walk of faith.

# Jacob

In order to understand the Holocaust, we need to examine some old spiritual issues of the Jews, about Israel as a country and as a nation. The answers lie in the past, and the Bible is our database.

The name "Israel" first appeared in the Bible when Jacob fought the angel in Genesis 32, so let us analyze that incident because that is the root of the nation of Israel and its walk of faith.

The Bible doesn't give us any evidence as to how or why the struggle started, just that they wrestled all night. But we do know that Jacob realized he was not fighting a normal human being. Yet he continued to fight.

If we put ourselves in Jacob's situation, most of us would kneel in respect and fear, and apologize upon realizing our opponent was an angel. Few of us would have the guts to ask for a blessing. But Jacob fought on and on, and even though the angel had caused damage to his hip, Jacob would not let go despite the pain he was suffering. The question is, "Why?"

Pride and tenacity are the answer. We see that Jacob had much pride in his physical strength. He alone was able to roll the stone away from the opening of the well in Genesis 29, showing off in front of Rachel. And he was not afraid of hard work to achieve his purposes, working seven years for Rachel and then later another seven years, but he lacked discernment and could not see Laban's maneuvering. He had confidence in his strength and in his ability to finish hard tasks. And he did not give up, even if doing so would have spared him physical suffering.

Jacob was not afraid to deceive his father to get the blessing (he was worried about how to accomplish it) and was not afraid to fight the angel for the blessing, either. He was the opposite of his father Isaac and his grandfather Abraham, who were more insecure and even lied regarding their wives, saying they were their sisters, for fear of their lives.

And his faith in the Lord is also quite different from the faith that Abraham and Isaac had. He made a vow in Genesis 28:20, which sounds like a secular Jew of today, saying out loud that if the Lord protects him on his journey, provides for him, and helps him to come back home safely, then he will believe. It is a conditional faith; meaning you give the Lord a condition, and if He meets it, fine, you will believe. But if He doesn't, you won't.

Whether we realize it or not, when we do that, we are elevating ourselves to a high position, equal to that of God. This comes from the fact that we were created in His image. "So God created man in His own image; in the image of God..." (Genesis 1:27).

By the way, here in the English translation, the word "image" appears twice, but in Hebrew those are two different words. The first word, "betzelmenu," means "in Our shadows." Which means that we are the shadow of the Light of the Lord on earth. The other word, "kedmutenu," means "like Our image." But we forget that we are only in His image and we start behaving like we are God.

This leads us to judge His actions. Like the scripture in Malachi 3:14 that says, "It is useless to serve God; What profit is it that we have kept His ordinance...?"

Again, the problem is that when the Lord does not do things the way we think He should, then we stop trusting Him and our faith is gone. It is an earthly kind of faith, meaning that if He helps us in our physical and financial issues, then we are willing to believe in Him and to obey Him.

Satan tried to use this reasoning when he approached God about Job, saying, "Does Job fear God for nothing?" (Job 1:9). He argued that Job only had faith in God because of the blessings of God in his life. The Lord wanted to show Satan that it was not so, and that is why Job went through the trial of losing everything, to see if he would also lose his faith because of it. Job passed the test and God blessed him even more in the latter days of his life.

In Genesis 28, Jacob had a dream. In the dream, the Lord tells Jacob that the land on which he lies He will give to him and his descendants, and that Jacob's descendants will spread in all directions, and the all the families of the earth will be blessed through them. And that He will be with him and protect him.

Jacob's reaction was that of a simple-minded person, disregarding everything the Lord had said about the land, his descendants, and the blessings to the whole earth. He only focused on his vow regarding his physical needs and returning home safely from his journey. The present situation was all that mattered to him as he was focused on survival. Sound familiar?

He disregarded the land, except that it was a gate of heaven, and put a rock to mark it and he went on without any further thoughts. His vow and his behavior showed he did not believe or even really hear or think about what the Lord had said. He just wanted to be taken care of, to survive.

Jacob did not pray to the Lord for provisions and a safe journey because he did not see Him as his God. He just made a vow, a conditional vow, that if He took care of him, then the Lord would be his God. He would not have even made that vow without having had the dream, because he always relied on himself and his self-confidence.

I just described here the basic character of Israel as a nation, as it was formed through Jacob after his struggle with the angel. Genesis 32:28 says, "Your name shall no longer be called Jacob, but Israel; for you have struggled with God and with men, and have prevailed." That was a prophecy that truly came to pass.

Throughout history, the Jews have shown again and again that they would not be easily subdued, nor would they accept another country's control over them, even if it was the Lord's will. "I will give all Judah into the hand of the king of Babylon..." (Jeremiah 20:4). Their will was more important than God's will.

And they have shown that being under the Lord's authority was hard for them. We talked about how they wanted a physical king, as shown in 1 Samuel 8:7, "...for they have not rejected you, but they have rejected Me, that I should not reign over them." This is because they wanted to be like all the other nations, and because they wanted a king they could see, not a king they could not see (God).

But back to Jacob. He did come to have the spiritual understanding that a new walk of faith was needed in order to go forward. In Genesis 35, he told his servants to purify themselves, change their garments, and to bury all their foreign idols in the ground. He realized this without the Lord telling him. That is exactly what we need to do nowadays!

New garments are a physical manifestation of a spiritual renewal. Jacob understood the importance of garments to a person's walk of faith. That may be the root as to why the religious Jews are so attached to their traditional black clothing and that it reminds them of their walk of faith.

It is similar to putting a mezuzah on your door. It reminds us of the Exodus and the blood on the doorposts. But in the Hebrew translation, Isaiah 57:8 says, "You have put your memory (of Me) behind the door and at the doorpost for you have removed yourself from Me..." The physical object of the mezuzah had become a replacement for a deep relationship with the Lord, but gave them a spiritual identity, as this scripture implies.

Should these things be done today? That is for you, the reader, to discern.

Our perception of the world plays a huge part in our walk of faith. Believers should have a different perception of the world from that of non-believers, otherwise the hardships of life will pull us away from the spirit, as we saw in the parable of the seeds in Matthew 13:22. "Now he who received seed among the thorns is he who hears the word, and the cares of this world and the deceitfulness of riches choke the word, and he becomes unfruitful."

So how should a believer see the world in order to stay on course spiritually, despite everyday hardships? What spiritual perception did the Jews in exile have before the Holocaust?

# Perception of Faith

After Adam and Eve ate from the tree of the knowledge of good and evil, the first thing that happened is that their perception changed.

Their now-sinful state could not exist in the perfect garden. They knew they were naked and tried to cover themselves, just as we try to cover our sins today.

Because they ate from the tree of the knowledge of good and evil, it was <u>for their benefit</u> to live in a different physical world that fit their new perception and reality.

Imagine living forever in that fallen state, with pain and difficulty in childbirth, toiling the cursed land forever, with no hope for the future, nothing ever changing, never getting older. It would have been a very tiring and depressing prospect.

There is comfort and strength for us, knowing that everything is temporary (even though, at the same time, we still strive to get to the point of comfort and security with no changes for the rest of our lives, forgetting that everything is temporary)!

We see now that what on the surface appeared to be God's punishment was actually His grace. However, Adam and Eve saw it and felt it as punishment. You can see their bitterness, especially Eve's, by the name she chose for their firstborn son, Cain, because she said she bought him from God. When you buy something, you need to pay for it. Her payment, I am sure she felt, was due to disobeying God.

We need to remember that when we suffer, we have to get beyond the physical reality, our feelings, and logical thinking in order to understand His will. The Bible helps us to do that.

The scripture in Romans 12:2 gives us more information as to how to accomplish it. "And do not be conformed to this world, but be transformed by the renewing of your mind, that you may prove (discern) what is that good and acceptable and perfect will of God."

We all have eyes and see the same things, but our perceptions and interpretations are not all the same. Even though we may talk about the same reality, the world still holds different meanings for each of us.

For example, to small animals such as the ant, the world seems vastly different than it does to us, and a simple lawn becomes an endless jungle. How we look at the world creates our reality, our world view. So how should we, as believers, look at the world?

The scripture in Luke 6:41 gives us further insight into that. Yeshua is asking us why we see the speck in our brother's eye and do not see the plank in our own eye. So He said that we should first remove the plank from our own eye and then we will be able to see clearly to remove the speck from our brother's eye.

Yeshua is saying here that, when looking at the world, our perception of it is distorted by the issues we have in ourselves, and it also affects how we handle the world. It can cause us to "not see the forest for the trees" or, as Yeshua called the religious Jews in Matthew 23:24, "Blind guides, who strain out a gnat and swallow a camel!"

The more we are detached from the world, or in Yeshua's words, "being in the world but not of the world," the more spiritual clarity we will have when looking at the world.

The perception of the believer lies in keeping the Lord in the center of our lives and discerning His will and His actions in the world by using the Bible as our guidebook and the Holy Spirit as our guide.

We can see whether we have faith or not when facing obstacles or crises, and that is why, in Luke 17:1, Yeshua says that obstacles must come. For example, in Matthew 14:28-31, we see that when Peter was still in the boat and saw Yeshua walking on the water, he felt that he could walk on the water, too. He was secure in that environment and thought his faith was strong. But as soon as he was out on the water facing the storm, his faith vanished, and Yeshua said to him, "O you of little faith, why did you doubt?"

When things are going well and we feel secure, we think we have strong faith, but it may be an illusion. So in order for us not to deceive ourselves, the Lord brings storms that will clearly show us where our faith really is, and we can easily perceive it. We must keep our focus on Him and not on the obstacles/hardships.

The nonbelievers are more attached to the things of the world and its activities and have no understanding of the spiritual world. They live in their own world, their own bubble, believing that is all there is to reality.

I was living in my own small world when I was in Japan. It was all about me, my studies, my desire to improve myself, and to get more control and discipline in my life. I had no faith in God, and people who were not part of my life did not really exist for me. I was in the center, everything was moving around me, and through my feelings I was connected to everything in my small world.

There is another perception of the world that is based on faith, which is that of the ultra-Orthodox Jews and some Christian denominations. I compare their walk of faith to that of a horse with blinders.

# A Horse with Blinders

"'O house of Israel, can I not do with you as this potter?' says the Lord." If we do not let our Lord mold us according to His will, then do we really have faith? Do we really trust Him?

Sometimes things happen in our lives in order to push us to do things that we should have done on our own but could not because we were like a horse with blinders – self-focused, seeing only what is directly in front of us, and missing the whole picture. Sometimes we do not want to see the whole picture because of the fear that we might have to make some changes, so we close our eyes and pretend that everything is fine.

So how can we break this self-focus? One way is by seeking or allowing changes in our lives so we can't remain on automatic pilot for too long. When we have the same routine, live in the same house, do the same job for years and years, we can end up fearing any kind of change because life has become very convenient and predictable. But the path of least resistance is not always best for our walk of faith.

We need changes in order to remain ourselves and not become robots. But many times, we find it is more comfortable and secure to live like a robot. I believe that is also one of the reasons why the Jews didn't want to leave Europe before the Holocaust. Fear of change.

I also saw this when I lived in Japan. Most people there are terrified of change and will do anything to keep things the way they are, even if they are suffering. They

32

won't rock the boat and they hate confrontation. That is why my Japanese boss told me that the secret to a long marriage is endurance, not love!

Change rips off the blinders and forces us to look at ourselves and at life from a different perspective in uncomfortable circumstances until we get used to the new pattern. A sense of continuity is essential to our feelings of security, and so we do everything to repair it when it is disrupted, as it was during the Coronavirus. Because of that, we don't understand the merit of having changes.

Change is so important that in Psalm 55:19 it says, "Because they do not change, therefore they do not fear God." This happens when we trust ourselves and our abilities to handle life through the power of habits and repetitions. There is no urgent need for God if all is going well, and we can continue our life without changes and without crying out to the Lord. But that brings complacency.

Here is another example of the need to change. If a man has the same job for twenty years, he has confidence in his abilities, and other people trust him to do the job because he is so experienced and successful at it. But what happens if he loses that job and winds up in another line of work that he is not confident in? He is on his toes every moment of the day, insecure in his abilities. Only then does he call upon the Lord for help.

It happened to me when I started to work for a company as a forklift driver. I had some experience with forklifts, but nothing like what I was supposed to do there, and it was absolutely nothing like the profession I had been in all my life. It can be a very dangerous job. So, every time I had to lift a big load up very high, I would cry out to the

Lord to help me. Never have I cried out to the Lord so intensely at work before.

Change is a part of life and God uses it for our benefit. Many times He is the one who brings about the change, such as the Holocaust.

Can the Jews' walk of faith during the 2,000 years in exile be seen as that of a horse with blinders? Let's examine that.

Attachment to the physical world is one cause of living like a horse with blinders and resisting change.

Unbelievers put their trust in the physical world. In the time of the Bible, their faith was in statues and pagan rituals. Nowadays, it is money, houses, power, etc. That is how the world operates. But as I said before, believers walk by faith, not by sight (2 Corinthians 5:7). That is how we break our attachment to the physical world.

The physical emphasis for the Jews was circumcision. Circumcision is a crucial factor in defining who is a Jew. If a man was circumcised, he was a Jew! That was it – end of story. But look at Jeremiah 9:26 that says, "For all these nations are uncircumcised, and all the house of Israel are uncircumcised in the heart."

We see that, in God's eyes, physical circumcision is not enough. Romans 2:29 says, "...but he is a Jew who is one inwardly; and circumcision is that of the heart, in the Spirit, not in the letter; whose praise is not from men but from God."

Physical things should not be what affects our spiritual walk, even things that are related to the Lord, such as the Holy Temple. But unfortunately, they do, as we will soon find out.

The Jews had put their trust in the Holy Temple in Jerusalem, and that is why they thought that nothing could happen to them and the city. Their faith was based on sight and not on a personal relationship and knowing the Lord.

That is why Jeremiah told them in Jeremiah 7:4, "Do not trust in these lying words, saying 'The temple of the Lord, the temple of the Lord, the temple of the Lord are these.'" In other words, don't trust in the Holy Temple to save you from your enemy. Don't put your trust in physical things.

It is similar to the attachment some Christians have to their church buildings. This became more evident during the Coronavirus, when restrictions that did not allow gathering in churches affected many people and their walk with the Lord.

Later, God instructed Jeremiah to tell the people, "Behold, I set before you the way of life and the way of death. He who remains in this city shall die by the sword, by famine, and by pestilence; but he who goes out and defects to the Chaldeans who besiege you, he shall live, and his life shall be as a prize to him. For I have set My face against this city for adversity and not for good,' says the Lord. 'It shall be given into the hand of the king of Babylon, and he shall burn it with fire.'" (Jeremiah 21:8-10).

God clearly warned them and gave them the choice of life or death. He told them the way for them to survive was to surrender to the Chaldeans. Yet they did not surrender, the Holy Temple was destroyed, and many people died or were sent to exile.

Why didn't they heed Jeremiah's word? Because they were so sure in their ways and their beliefs that they did not think it would really happen. They did not see what was going on around them, like a horse with blinders, and they were deaf to the warning calls to change direction. Being stubborn and stiff-necked, as the Lord described His people, didn't help matters. A stiff neck happens when we are stuck in one direction for a long period of time. For example, when we drive on the highway for hours, we get a stiff neck because we are just looking ahead for a long time, going in one direction.

That is one reason why the people of Israel were so devastated when the Holy Temple was destroyed. There was no longer spiritual security and assurance in their walk because it was based on a physical structure.

Self-focus, not listening to the Lord, and preferring to go their own way even if it meant to die rather than to be slaves, as we saw in Masada, was the Jews' way of thinking. Their own thoughts and feelings came first, before the Lord's will and instructions.

I was the same way before I came to know the Lord. I had recently met my beloved and we were shopping at a supermarket. I was very tired and focused on the task at hand and in a hurry to just get home and relax. At the checkout, my beloved was talking with the cashier while I was basically "checked out" and waiting to leave.

Afterward, she turned to me and asked why I did not say anything to the guy at the register. I realized that he did not really exist for me as I did not pay him any attention. That's when she said to me, "The Lord put him in our path, and you did not acknowledge him."

At first, I did not understand why she was making a big deal out of that guy, a total stranger, a cashier, someone you pass by a few times every week without giving him or her much thought. It was the same with the security guards. I was so self-focused that I did not acknowledge their existence. There was no merit in talking with them, my logical mind told me. I was like a horse with blinders, just seeing my way and what was essential to me.

This was such an important and much-needed lesson for me. Now that I have acknowledged the Lord and His ways in my life, I consider every person that comes across my path, not ignoring them or taking them for granted, because the Lord may have put him or her in my path for His purposes.

We see only the here-and-now, while the Lord knows the future, and we need to trust Him that He knows what is best for us. That is faith.

Jeremiah describes it in 11:8. "Yet they did not obey (hear) or incline their ear (pay attention), but everyone followed the dictates of his evil heart;" You see what stopped them from hearing the Lord? Their self-focus!

When we follow our own hearts and our own agenda, then we do not hear the Lord. We may have obstacles in our lives without understanding why and just see them as ordinary hardships, but sometimes God puts them there because of our issues.

Again, Jeremiah 6:19 says, "Behold, I will certainly bring calamity on this people – the fruit of their thoughts, because they have not heeded My words nor My law, but rejected it." And verse 21 says, "Behold, I will lay stumbling blocks before this people…"

The Lord has always given Israel a warning before releasing a calamity upon them. The problem was, and still is, a lack of discernment regarding the warnings, and their unwillingness to make changes in their lives or in their way of thinking. Stiffness of character.

That is what happens when your faith has a shaky foundation, and you are not even aware of it.

Sometimes, even the greatest leaders could not save the people of Israel because of their sins. "Even if Moses and Samuel stood before Me, My mind would not be favorable toward this people." (Jeremiah 15:1).

Another component of the physical world that affects our walk is the issue of security, and that can cause us to walk with blinders.

For many of us, security is strengthened by numbers. When many people are united in thought, they have the feeling of security. Crowd mentality. Safety in numbers. It is a very natural thing for human beings.

We see it in the Holocaust, too. It was easier to walk with everybody than to venture out on your own and try to escape.

That is also one of the reasons the Jews always lived together in communities during their centuries of exile. Spiritual security is connected to physical security, and it is strengthened when in numbers.

This is reinforced when people are more connected to their leaders, the rabbis, than to God, and love the praise of men more than the praise of God, as the scripture in John 12:43 says.

One of the results of walking with blinders is that when our trust is in our leaders, kings, or rabbis, then we will suffer when they make mistakes, even if we are righteous, as in the example in 1 Kings 20:42 when the prophet says to the king, "Thus says the Lord: 'Because you have let slip out of your hand a man whom I appointed to utter destruction, therefore your life shall go for his life, and your people for his people.'" He was referring to the king of the Syrians, Hadad. King Ahab made a peace covenant with the enemy instead of obeying the Lord.

Now, peace sounds great, and we all want that, especially with our enemies, but you see that if it is not according to God's will, then the people of Israel will suffer because of it.

There is another reason why the Jews' walk of faith was in one direction, without looking around them, and that is the role of the Jewish women in the Jewish men's walk of faith. The role of a woman in Jewish religion has nothing to do with spiritual direction.

But in Jeremiah 31:22, it says, "For the Lord has created a new thing in the earth – a woman shall encompass a man." The Hebrew translation is "a woman shall turn a man around."

I was curious as to why this verse about women was included in such an important chapter about the new covenant and the time after the destruction of Jerusalem and the return of the Jews to their land from exile.

In order to understand this, we need to get to the root of the woman's spiritual walk.

Hebrews 12:29 says, "For our God is a consuming fire." Since we were created in His image (Genesis 1:26), then it follows that we would have His fire in us. The word for "fire" in Hebrew is "esh" (Aleph, Shin). The Hebrew words for "man" and "woman" both contain the word "fire."

39

The Hebrew words in Genesis 2:23 show us that this is indeed true.

But there is a difference in how the fire of God manifests in men and women. This is evident even in the way the words are spelled. "Man" in Hebrew is "ish" (Aleph, Yod, Shin), and "woman" in Hebrew is "ishah" (Aleph, Shin, Hay).

In "man" you see that the two letters of fire are not together, they are divided by the Yod, because the fire in man is divided. One side is earthly and the other side is spiritual.

Fire requires a physical substance, such as wood, and a nonphysical substance, air, in order to burn. We can see this in everyday life. Men are concerned with physical, earthly achievement and with spiritual direction, as well.

In the word "woman" in Hebrew, the two letters of fire are right next to each other, with the added letter "Hay" after them. The letter "Hay" represents God. Again, that is the letter which God added to Abram's name and he became Abraham, and to Sarai's name and she became Sarah.

The fact that the fire in woman is not divided like it is in man means that she is naturally more focused on the Lord and flows more easily with Him.

Going back to Jeremiah, we see that before the destruction of the Holy Temple, the woman was just following the man in everything. But because of the future destruction of the temple, the Lord knew that the Jews would have a problem finding their way spiritually, since the temple was the physical as well as the spiritual heart of the Jews' faith. I believe that's why God put the scripture about women in the chapter regarding the spiritual future of Israel.

Man now needed the woman's spiritual input for the direction that he should take, and so Jeremiah 31:22 tells us that a woman will be able to turn around the man's spiritual walk, which will result in changing the direction of his physical walk as well.

I personally can attest to that, as I was so self-focused on finding "the way" through martial arts in Japan, yet wound up finding the true Way, Yeshua, through a woman named Deborah, who is now my wife. She literally turned my direction around spiritually and physically.

In Genesis 2:18, we see another purpose for Eve. The Lord said, "It is not good that man should be alone; I will make him a helper comparable to him."

If we think that the Lord had created Eve just for the physical or mental aspects of Adam being alone, then we cut God short. There is always a spiritual aspect, as well, and this is explained in the second part of the scripture where he talks about her as a helper.

The Hebrew goes much deeper. Part of the word means helper, but the other part means "against." That is confusing! How can Eve be a helper and yet be against him?

The answer lies in a deeper spiritual understanding of Adam and Eve and their nature. Adam is active, while Eve has a passive, opposite nature.

Most men will tell you that they don't feel manly when they are passive. They need to be active to feel they are men, and men tend to have their way of doing things. Eve, the woman, helps the man to learn to be passive in order to follow the Lord and His way, not the man's way.

For example, before the destruction of the first temple, Jeremiah gave the people of Israel two choices: be

41

active, fight the enemy, and die; or be passive, surrender, and live. The Lord did not want His people to die, but to be passive, surrender, and live.

Jeremiah 27:13 says, "Why will you die, you and your people, by the sword, by the famine, and by the pestilence, as the Lord has spoken against the nation that will not serve the king of Babylon?" But my people decided to be active and fight, even though the Lord wanted them to be passive and surrender.

How important it is, then, to know when to be passive and accept His will and His direction, and Eve was created to help Adam do that.

Patience is the ability to be passive in everyday life, and so when Eve (the woman) helps Adam (the man) to be passive, she helps him to have patience and to wait on the Lord – provided she walks in the Spirit, of course!

Without the spiritual input and direction of women after the destruction of the first and second temples, the Jews' walk of faith became like that of a horse with blinders, reflecting a man that is self-focused spiritually and physically.

I believe another reason we live our life like a horse with blinders is lack of self-examination. We cannot say we believe in Yeshua and leave it at that.

Scripture commands us, "Examine yourselves as to whether you are in the faith. Test yourselves. Do you not know yourselves, that Jesus Christ (Yeshua) is in you?" (2 Corinthians 13:5).

And I also love Galations 2:20, "… it is no longer I who live, but Christ (Yeshua) lives in me…"

So we need to question our thoughts and actions and ask ourselves, "Would Yeshua think like that or act like that?"

The need to examine ourselves is crucial, as we tend to let our habits justify a convenient way of life for us. We put ourselves in a box without even noticing it unless we examine ourselves.

Isaiah 1:3 says, "The ox knows its owner and the donkey its master's crib; but Israel does not know, My people do not consider." The Hebrew translation is "…My people do not <u>examine</u>." It is not only to examine your own walk, but also to examine what is around you and to discern the Lord's work in your life and in other people's lives.

When we do not examine ourselves, we deceive ourselves, and end up not knowing God. Jeremiah 9:6 says, "'Through deceit they refuse to know Me', says the Lord." (Regarding the people of Israel.)

We may also be deceived by others whom we may think are spiritual and have authority. An example of that is the story in 1 Kings Chapter 13, the story about the man of God and the old prophet. The man of God stayed true to the word of the Lord against the king, but on his way back, the old prophet went to meet him. He lied to the man of God, who was deceived by the fact that the prophet was old and had said the angel of God told him to invite the man of God to his house. The man of God went, disobeying what the Lord Himself had spoken to him directly, and he subsequently paid with his life because of it.

A sad story, and frightening as well, that your worst enemy can be someone who professes to be a believer like you, but is actually a wolf in sheep's clothing.

Another issue of having blinders is the focus on works in order to reach righteousness, and not on faith. "…but Israel, pursuing the law of righteousness, has not attained to the law of righteousness. Why? Because they did not seek it by faith, but as it were, by the works of the law." (Romans 9:31-32).

It was evident even at Mt. Sinai when the Israelites told Moses that they will do and then they will hear, in Exodus 24:7. From that moment on, the Jews have seen their spiritual identity according to their doings and not by faith.

However, James 1:23-24 tells us that works related to faith are important. "For if anyone is a hearer of the word and not a doer, he is like a man observing his natural face in a mirror; for he observes himself, goes away, and immediately forgets what kind of man he was."

But we are talking about deeds that are reflecting your faith, not deeds that are reflecting your desire for righteousness. It is important to see the difference.

When works become the most spiritually important thing, it puts a huge burden on the people, causing them to only look ahead to the next works they have to do. It reminds me of when they made us march in the army for hours on end. After a few kilometers, you stop looking sideways or around you because you have no energy for that. You can only look ahead to the next step and you can become vulnerable to the enemy.

We can also become deceived when we put God in a box of our own thinking. Malachi 3:8 says, "Will a man fixate God?" (This is the Hebrew translation - In English the word "rob" is used). Yet you have fixated Me! But you say 'In what way have we fixated You? In tithes and offerings.'"

A Horse with Blinders

The people of Israel had God fixed in their way of thinking, that if you give tithes and offerings, then you are spiritually covered and do not need to worry about your spiritual walk, or whether you are hearing the Lord.

How should our faith be built so that we will have a solid spiritual walk without deceiving ourselves?

# The Foundation of Faith

Faith, whether it is Christian, Messianic, or Jewish, should be based on the desire to have a relationship with the Lord. That is why the first commandment is, as we see in Mark 12:30, "And you shall love the Lord your God with all your heart, with all your soul, with all your mind, and with all your strength." Moses had also said in Deuteronomy 6:5, "You shall love the Lord your God with all your heart, with all your soul, and with all your strength."

When I examine myself, I realize that I don't always love the Lord with all my soul or my mind because the issues of life affect me, temporarily, and I don't act in the spirit but out of my old self.

When we fulfill the first commandment, we put Him in the center of our lives and not ourselves, and that is the foundation of faith. Again, for us to do that, we need to let go of our control, of our being in the center. Only then will we know God. As I mentioned earlier, Psalm 46:10 says, "Let go and know that I am God." (Hebrew translation).

Further explanation of letting go of the control of our lives is seen in Romans 6:6-7 where it says, "...our old man was crucified with Him, that the body of sin might be done away with, that we should no longer be slaves of sin. For he who has died has been freed from sin." We should see ourselves as dead to sin, but alive to God in Yeshua, the Messiah, our Lord.

It means that we do not let the body control us with its desires. The Lord said in Genesis 4:7, "If you do well, will you not be accepted? And if you do not do well, sin lies at the door. And its desire is for you, but you should rule over it." In Hebrew, this scripture says, "If you do well or if you do not do well, sin lies at the door and to you, its desire, and you will rule over it."

The Lord is telling Cain that the real issue is not whether your actions are good enough or not, but it is how you control the desires and temptations that are at the door that lead to sin, and that you can control your desires. That is what Cain should focus on. That is what we must keep in mind, also, that good deeds will not save us from the temptations at the door.

It is interesting that sin lies at the door, and in Exodus the Hebrews needed to put blood on the doorpost. The blood covered their sins.

Another issue of our foundation of faith is the fear of the Lord, which I will write about later in more detail. If that fear would be a more real, daily substance of our walk of faith, it would stop our indulgence of the flesh. That is why the scripture in Jeremiah 32:39 says, "…I will give them one heart and one way, that they may fear Me forever…"

It is important for us to understand for our walk of faith that it was necessary for Yeshua to come to earth before the second temple was destroyed because the Jews needed a new spiritual way of life once it was destroyed. He came just for that reason, at that time in history, to show the Jews the way to the Father that was not based on the Holy Temple, because they had misused it.

Again, Isaiah 5:12 says, "But they do not regard the work of the Lord, nor consider the operation of His hands." We need to focus on His power and discern His works in our midst every day, not just recall past events like the Holocaust and the Exodus.

The next verse tells us what happened because they did not do that. "Therefore my people have gone into captivity, because they have no knowledge." Doesn't that remind you of the Holocaust? Life changed in a moment for the Jews in Europe and they did not understand why it happened and where God was!

So how does God want us to walk? Genesis 17:1 gives us a huge hint about a fundamental issue of our faith when the Lord tells Abraham, "…walk before Me and be innocent." This is the Hebrew translation. The English translation is "blameless."

This is also seen in Job 1:8 when God says, "Have you considered My servant Job, that there is none like him on the earth, an innocent (not blameless) man, straight, one who fears God and shuns evil?" (Hebrew).

Right there you can see that one of the qualities the Lord wants us to have as a foundation of faith is the innocence of a child. Yeshua said in Luke 18:17, "…whoever does not receive the kingdom of God as a little child will by no means enter it." He is not demanding us to be perfect.

The next characteristic of Job is that he is "straight." The Old Testament gives us a lot of information as to how to have security in God. When we do what is right in His eyes, He will send a warning if calamity is coming. The Hebrew translation for doing right in His eyes, as you see, for example, in 2 Kings 12:2 or 2 Kings 18:3, is to do "straight" in His eyes. The word "yashar" means straight.

The Hebrew word for "Israel" is literally "straight God," a nation that does what is right in God's eyes and follows Him closely. They are aligned "straight" with Him. When the Jews did evil in the sight of the Lord, they wandered far from Him, ceased to exist as a nation, and the people went into exile.

The only tribe in Israel that contains the Hebrew letters for "straight" is the tribe of Issachar. If you take the first, third and fifth letters, you get the word in Hebrew "yashar."

What is special about the tribe of Issachar? The answer is in 1 Chronicles 12:32, "...the sons of Issachar who had understanding of the times, to know what Israel ought to do..." When you understand what is happening around you and know the timing of the Lord in those things, you know the best route to move forward – straight – without detours or sidetracks that happen when you don't make decisions according to His timing and instructions.

Another example of how important it is to know His timing as an essential part of the foundation of faith is in the story of the ten virgins (Matthew 25:1-13) who waited with their oil lamps for the Lord to come. The Lord came, but five of the women were not there, as they had gone to buy oil because they had none. Later, when they knocked on the door, the Lord didn't merely say, "Sorry, you're late and missed the boat." He said, "Assuredly, I say to you, I do not know you."

There is such an important warning here. When you don't know His timing, or you are not ready for Him because you are busy with your own issues, it can lead to hearing those same words. Because to know Him means you have a close relationship with Him.

The nation of Israel originated in the book of Exodus when the Hebrews left slavery and began to live as a nation of free men and women following the Lord. Therefore, we need to examine Exodus as to the Hebrews' walk of faith and what we can learn from them today in our walk.

By the way, Holocaust Memorial Day in Israel is usually within two weeks of Passover (Exodus). Is it a coincidence? That is for you the reader to find out.

# Exodus

The word "exodus" has another meaning in Hebrew, and that is "destruction" (same letters, but the pronunciation is different). The Holocaust was the destruction of the Jews' way of life in Europe. In the Bible, it is about the destruction of Egypt and of the old life of the Hebrews as slaves.

We need to ask ourselves why the process of the Exodus took such a long time and involved such dramatic displays of the power of God. God could have softened Pharaoh's heart in a second and the Jews could have been released right away, fast and easy, the way we like things done, especially in our fast-moving society of today. And the longer it took to get them out of Egypt, the more the Jews suffered. So why didn't the Lord take the fast, easy way for the Exodus?

The reason for it is that the faith of the Jews had to be formed. They had to be convinced of God's power over every aspect of life – over nature, gods, animals, and the power of life and death. Without the plagues, they would not have been so convinced. Without seeing His power, they would not have walked out of Egypt and into the unknown desert. For slaves, it would have been a death sentence to go wandering in the desert without the guidance of the Egyptians.

After all, they had been slaves for over 400 years. They had deep roots in Egypt as slaves and a deep-rooted slave mentality. They were used to being taken care of. They had the security of lodging and food in exchange for their hard work.

This is parallel to the way the Jews viewed the Nazis, believing that they needed them to work and so they would not kill them but provide for them. The Jews' roots in Europe were deep as well, especially in Poland.

My beloved and I went to the Jewish Museum in Warsaw and saw that the roots of the Jews there dated back to the 11th century. That is why 90% of the three million Jews in Poland died in the Holocaust. They had become so accustomed to life and the culture in Poland that they considered themselves loyal Poles who would never need to worry about persecution.

Since the Hebrews had lived in Egypt for so long, it is safe to assume that they followed the gods of the Egyptians. If you have doubts about that, then just read the book of Judges in the Bible and see how often the Israelites went after foreign gods. They wanted to follow gods that could be seen, which is contradictory to the God of Abraham, Isaac, and Jacob.

The Lord had to show the Egyptians and the Hebrews that He was more powerful than their gods. It had to be demonstrated physically, not just in words, because the Hebrews did not know God.

It is interesting that later in Exodus, the Lord tells the Hebrews, through Moses, to put blood over their doorposts - to cover over the sins that are at the door.

It is also interesting that the shape of a doorpost is the same shape as the Hebrew letter "Chet." The way we pronounce this letter is also the way we pronounce the word "sin" in Hebrew. The blood of the lamb covered their sins. And Yeshua is called the sacrificial lamb!

The Hebrews also needed to suffer much, enough to make them want to get out of Egypt. Without the suffering, they would have wanted to stay in Egypt in the security they had known rather than going into the desert, to the unknown, to probable death, for they had no knowledge of how to live in the desert.

It was the same during the Holocaust. The Jews in Europe would not have chosen to come to Israel before life had become so hard under the Nazis. Israel was not a developed country, and so to move there required hard physical work and the reality of facing danger from the Arabs. They did not want to risk the security they believed they had in the progressed countries of Europe.

In both instances, they did not have faith like Abraham to be able to leave everything they knew and go to the Promised Land.

The Hebrews were slaves. They learned to rely on other men, the Egyptians, for their lives, and they did not know God. They were bound physically, mentally, and spiritually to the Egyptians, just as the Jews were bound by the comforts of the world in Europe.

If we apply this principal to our everyday life today, we need to focus on God's power that can break the bondages we have with the old self that give us false security in our flesh and our own thinking. Sometimes we must endure suffering in order to let go of trusting in ourselves and the control that we think we have over our lives.

We need to remember that they were slaves and would not have had many assets, so to sacrifice a precious lamb would have been a big deal. It would have shown that they were willing to give of themselves as an act of obedience to the Lord. They had to demonstrate that they were convinced, not just in their thoughts, but also in their actions. They were no longer just passive spectators of the plagues that the Lord had hit Egypt with.

Until the last plague, the Hebrews did not have to do anything but watch. After all, if they could not publicly show their obedience to God by sacrificing something dear to them and putting the blood on the doorposts for everyone to see, then they would not really be willing to follow Moses out of Egypt and into the desert.

So, it was an act to unite the Jews under Moses before they left Egypt. The Lord knew that the Jews were (and still are) stubborn and difficult to lead and would cause trouble if things did not go the way they thought they should. That was one reason why the Lord had Moses instruct them to do that.

After leaving Egypt, God knew that the Jews needed something tangible to see that He was with them. First it was the Tabernacle, then it was the Ark of the Covenant, and then the Holy Temple. He also used the pillar of cloud by day and the pillar of fire at night to guide them. Why?

For their spiritual security, and because they had seen that the Egyptian gods all had physical forms, idols, so they expected a physical form from the God of Abraham, Isaac, and Jacob as well.

Look at what happened when Moses did not come back from Mt. Sinai. Moses was the physical entity that gave the Israelites their spiritual security throughout their sojourn in the desert. When he did not come back, they could not stay focused on God, and made a golden calf like they had seen in Egypt, in order to regain their spiritual security.

When we go through times of insecurity, we all look back and long for the times when we were secure and at peace. They suffered as slaves, but at least they felt secure.

The Jews in Europe had suffered so many persecutions before the Holocaust that they had to move from country to country for security. But very few went to Israel at that time. Once they had found security in places like Poland and other countries in Europe, it was very difficult for them to leave those places of security for the sake of moving to Israel, which was not so comfortable.

We always want to go back to comfort when times get hard. That is why every time the Israelites faced a problem in the desert such as lack of water or food, they immediately recalled the times in Egypt.

We need to remember that every time the Israelites experienced hard times in the desert, they wanted to return to Egypt. We must not do the same. Yeshua said in Luke 9:62, "No one, having put his hand to the plow, and looking back, is fit for the kingdom of God."

We see this in Exodus 16:3 when they complained to Moses for the lack of food, "And the children of Israel said to them, 'Oh that we had died by the hand of the Lord in the land of Egypt, when we sat by the pots of meat and when we ate bread to the full! For you have brought us out into this wilderness to kill this whole assembly with hunger.'"

Even we, during the Coronavirus, faced times of insecurity and we dreamed of going back to the wonderful days without masks and isolation.

So we see it is a very human thing to do, but spiritually we need to go beyond our human desires and focus on the Lord and His plan.

When Peter rebuked Yeshua in Matthew 16:22, it was because he was acting in a very human way when he heard Yeshua saying that He was going to suffer and be killed. Peter said, "Far be it from You, Lord; this shall not happen to You!"

We can totally understand Peter's behavior. But Yeshua's reaction was not what we would expect when Peter was expressing such compassion and protectiveness. In verse 23, He said, "Get behind Me, Satan! You are an offense to Me, for you are not mindful of the things of God, but of the things of men."

Yeshua makes it clear to us that if we focus on our human side and the things of men, we may actually wind up being against the Lord, taking sides with Satan unintentionally.

The Jews in Europe needed to be totally convinced that they must return to Israel and build a nation so that another Holocaust would never happen again, as you can read more about later in the chapter about Oct 7, 2023. They had to leave the many years of security that they enjoyed in Europe, even though that security was temporary due to local persecution.

After the Exodus, when the Israelites were in the desert and they heard the report of the ten spies, they said, "Let us select a leader and return to Egypt." (Numbers 14:4). When facing danger, the Jews looked back and remembered the security they felt in Egypt. They wanted to choose a leader who would lead them back to Egypt. Going against the Lord and His servant Moses was more than God could tolerate. Therefore, they were punished by going through the desert for forty years and those above the age of twenty died there without reaching their original destination, Israel.

This is a lesson for our generation that we need to learn and remember. If we rely only on what we know, on what gives us security and comfort, on physical things when facing danger, and not on God, we will be disciplined. Because, practically speaking, when we don't trust Him, even if we say that we believe in Him, we are actually acting like a non-believer.

Was the exodus from Egypt a success? Leaving Egypt was a huge accomplishment, going from bondage to freedom. But the journey wasn't supposed to stop there. They had an ultimate destination, to come to the Promised Land. Tradition will keep you from focusing on your destination (I will elaborate on tradition later), as we see in Passover celebrations.

Obviously, the generation of those who left Egypt did not reach their destination, but the new generation that was born in the desert did. The Lord said in Numbers 14:29, "The carcasses of you who have complained against Me shall fall in this wilderness, all of you who were numbered, according to your entire number, from twenty years old and above." Joshua and Caleb were the only exceptions.

So, according to the Lord, anyone who is twenty or above is considered an adult, someone whose voice is to be considered (a complaint in this case), and those younger than twenty are not to be taken to account due to lack of maturity, male and female.

In Japan, the ceremony of young men and women of becoming adults is at the age of twenty. Interesting! But in Israel, it is the age of thirteen for boys and twelve for girls.

From that, we can also see that the Lord did not want any men or women over the age of sixty to enter and settle in the Promised Land, if you add up the forty years in the desert. Again, except for Joshua and Caleb.

In Numbers 16, we see the revolt of Korah and his people against Moses. Here we can learn another lesson regarding faith. Moses told them in Numbers 16:5, "…Tomorrow morning the Lord will show who is His and who is holy, and will cause (choose) him to come near to Him."

This reminds me of Cain and Abel, who both gave offerings to the Lord. The Lord chooses who He acknowledges and who He does not. The one the Lord acknowledges is the one the Lord will bring close to Him, as in this case.

We can also see it among the religious Jews, when they are so consumed with all the things they have to do, that there is no relationship with the Lord.

The Lord shows here a difference between being holy and being close to Him. I think many of us, Christians and Jews, would be content to be considered holy, but you see that it is not enough for the Lord.

Aaron and Miriam made a similar assumption in Numbers 12:1-2, "Then Miriam and Aaron spoke against Moses (as Korah did) because of the Ethiopian woman whom he had married…they said, 'Has the Lord indeed spoken only through Moses? Has He not spoken through us also?' And the Lord heard it."

We see that the Lord was angry at Miriam and Aaron for saying that, and came to Moses' defense. In verses 12:6-9, the Lord describes His relationship with Moses as closer than with any other human being. When they complained against Moses and his behavior, they were, in fact, criticizing the Lord and His choice of putting Moses as the leader. That is why the Lord was angry at them. Moses was closer to God than any other person.

The Lord wants a close relationship with us, like that of a husband and wife. Hosea 2:20 says, "I will betroth you to Me in faithfulness, and you shall know the Lord." But if we are satisfied with being holy, being the chosen people of the Lord, it will not help us to survive – not in the desert (the Israelites), nor in Europe during the Holocaust.

The Lord showed the Jews in Europe that being the chosen people could be a burden if you are content with only that, and not close enough to the Lord to know His will, His plan.

We see it also in the book of Esther. It was a warning of what might happen in the future, and it came to pass in the Holocaust.

We see in the Book of Esther that Haman, the evil man that was in a position of high authority, managed to convince the king, Ahasuerus, to give the order to kill and annihilate all the Jews, both young and old, little children and women (Esther 3:13). This is parallel to the Holocaust, with Hitler's plan to exterminate all the Jews.

Mordecai told Esther, who was Jewish, the queen at that time, about the plan and convinced her to change the king's command.

So, in the end, Haman was punished and died in the same way that he had planned to kill Mordecai, and the Jews were saved. It is an amazing story, and you should all read the Book of Esther.

Unfortunately, things did not go smoothly for the Jews in Europe during the Second World War.

When I was a child, I asked my mother, "Why did the Lord let the Holocaust happen?" I did not receive an answer that gave me peace. I am sure I was not the only one who had asked that question as a child. And now, as an adult, I talk with many people to get their opinions.

# People's Opinions about the Holocaust

One of the most common questions the Jews have asked during and after the Holocaust is, "Where was God?" or, "Where is God?"

I will ask a different question: "Where were the Jews?" How could they have not seen evil was coming? Why did they not discern the coming destruction? Where was their faith? What were the rabbis saying? Did the Lord our God just decide to bring such a calamity on His people without a warning? Has He ever done that in the Bible?

If you go through the Bible, you find out that the Lord always gives a warning and explains why a calamity was about to come, since it came from the Lord. Amos 3:6 says, "If there is calamity in a city, will not the Lord have done it?"

The problem is that the people of Israel, then and now, don't always see the whole picture. Just like Gideon in Judges 6:13 when he asked the angel of God, "...if the Lord is with us, why then has all this happened to us? And where are all His miracles which our fathers told us about, saying 'Did not the Lord bring us up from Egypt?' But now the Lord has forsaken us and delivered us into the hands of the Midianites." He asked the same question that the Jews asked during the Holocaust.

Gideon does not seem to be aware that "...the children of Israel did evil in the sight of the Lord. So the Lord delivered them into the hand of Midian for seven years, and the hand of Midian prevailed against Israel" (Judges 6:1-2).

If he did know it, maybe he did not make the connection between their suffering from Midian and the fact that the people of Israel were worshipping idols. He only focused on the miracles of God, even though God had sent a prophet to explain why they were suffering, in verses 8-10, who said it was because they had not obeyed God's voice.

And the Jews in Europe did get a warning of the calamity that was to come upon them. In fact, there were people, like Jabotinsky, an Israeli Zionist leader, who came to Europe and warned the Jews about a destruction that was to come.

In 1936, Jabotinsky met with three high officers in Poland, Hungary, and Romania with a plan to evacuate the total Jewish population of these countries to Israel. All three leaders agreed to the plan, but the resistance came from the Jews!

The Second World War started in 1939, so if the Jews in those countries had agreed with Jabotinsky's plan, then more than half of the Jews who died in the Holocaust would have been spared.

In 1938, Jabotinsky said the Polish Jews in Europe were living on the edge of a volcano. Later, in his speeches around Europe, he warned the Jews in Central and Eastern Europe of violent pogroms that were soon to come. He encouraged the Jews to leave Europe and come to Israel.

Most of the Jews in Europe did not heed the words of Jabotinsky at that time regarding the Holocaust approaching Europe. They did not heed his words due to self-focus, lack of discernment, and lack of belief that the

Germans would really harm them. (I will elaborate more about Jabotinsky later.) They considered their citizenship in Germany or Poland more important than belonging to the land that the Lord had given to their fathers.

When you do not heed the urgency of the Lord's warning, and then later on try to get out of the situation, it is not as easy as it would have been if you had heeded His timing. That is what happened in the Holocaust. Later on, when the Jews did want to leave and come to Israel, it was not easy. In 1939, the Second World War started, and that same year, the British had restricted the immigration of Jews to Israel to seventy-five thousand people per year.

One opinion that I heard from the Jews I had asked is that the six million Jews who died in the Holocaust were like a sacrifice for the sins of the Jews that turned their back to their religion and became like the Germans.

Where do we see such a thing in the Bible? The opposite is true. It says in 2 Kings 14:6, "...a person shall be put to death for his own sin." So, this way of thinking does not line up with the Bible. Also, in Ezekiel 18:20, it says, "The son shall not bear the guilt of the father, nor the father bear the guilt of the son." So the religious Jews in Europe were not punished because of the secular Jews who became like Germans.

Such thinking does not take into consideration that maybe we need to consider the actions of the Jews in Europe and try to find out if something was wrong in their walk of faith that they did not see it coming.

Moreover, in Ezekiel 21:3, the Lord says, "Behold, I am against you, and I will draw My sword out of its sheath and cut off both righteous and wicked from you." That is why innocent and righteous people, as well, died in the Holocaust.

When I ask people what we have learned spiritually from the Holocaust, or what the Jews have changed in their walk of faith after the Holocaust, the answer is, "Nothing." Nothing changed. As if the walk of faith of the Jews in Europe had been perfect prior to the Holocaust and still is up to this day! They say it was all the Germans' fault, period. They focus on how we were victims, and that is the end of the story, saying that Satan was using the Germans to annihilate the Jews.

But then where was God in all this? Just sightseeing? As if the Lord had a passive role in the Holocaust.

Another common opinion regarding the reason for the Holocaust is, "It is the Lord's will," meaning we simply cannot always understand the events in our lives.

From all that I've written so far about faith, we know that the Lord wants a deep relationship with us, and that He always sends prophets or messengers to deliver His warnings and gives the people of Israel time to repent and change their ways, as you see in the Bible. I will elaborate on the Lord's will in another chapter.

I want to believe that if I had been alive during the Holocaust I would have behaved differently, but I wonder if that truly would have been so. I wonder, because in my own life, I know I would not have left Japan after living there for twenty years if my life had not become unbearable. I loved Japan, but circumstances were closing in on me and I realized it was time to come back home. That is why I cannot say for sure that I would have heeded Jabotinsky's words, as a non-believer.

# If I Were in the Holocaust

While writing this book, I experienced an incident that showed me what I would have done if I had been in the Holocaust, and it was with the help of my beloved wife that I came to that realization.

We were in bed one night, trying to sleep, when we heard people talking quite loudly outside. It was employees from the pizza place near us who were hanging out with their friends in the street. It was after 10:00 at night. It bothered my beloved and she wanted me to go tell them to be quiet. I told her that it wasn't really late enough or serious enough to do that, and that we should just try to ignore it and go to sleep. Of course, I fell asleep right away because I can sleep through anything!

The next morning, my beloved told me that I was wrong about it and that I shouldn't have just ignored it. The Lord showed her that many Jews ignored the warnings and signs before the Holocaust and went like sheep to the slaughter. But then there were some who saw what was happening and tried to do something about it. They joined the Resistance, fought against the Nazis, and many lost their lives in the process. But at least they were willing to try to do something about it.

Which side should we choose to be on, even though we would most likely face death either way? She told me that we must be on the side of the resistance fighters! We must never have an attitude of "We will just endure," but we must choose life over death. Only the Lord knows the outcome, but He would see us choose life or He would make a way of escape. Like in Jeremiah 21:8-9 when the Lord said, "Behold, I set before you the way of life and the way of death. He who remains in this city shall die..." only in this case it was Europe.

My small example of ignoring the noise outside our window is nothing compared to the Holocaust, but God used it to bring me to the place where I had to ask myself what I would have done. Would I have joined the Resistance, or would I have just ignored the signs and gone with the flow all the way to the ovens? So many had no idea what was happening to them as they got in line, but there were some who realized they had to fight to the end or escape to Israel.

God can use even the smallest circumstance to teach us a huge lesson. In my case, it was a noisy pizza parlor that taught me that I cannot just endure and let it pass. My wife heard the Holy Spirit and brought me to the mirror where I saw my own heart. It was the perfect way to reveal to me how easy it can be to want to be comfortable, roll over, and just endure.

I also learned that my logical mind can talk me out of taking action and justify my being passive. This lesson hit me hard. I had always thought of myself as a fighter, and learning martial arts was my way of carrying out this fighting spirit. But even with my martial arts training, I was using my logic to just roll over and shut myself in. My wife is an example of a true warrior in every sense, and I am so grateful to her for showing me not to be passive.

When I became born again, I came to realize that one of the things that hinders the Jews from accepting Yeshua is that they think too much. The Jews have very sharp minds, but the price they pay for it is that they rely on their brains more than their hearts and cannot comprehend Yeshua's message, as it is based on love and humility.

And His message is simple, maybe too simple for the intellectual mind, as we see in 2 Corinthians 11:3, "But I fear, lest somehow, as the serpent deceived Eve by his craftiness, so your minds may be corrupted from the simplicity that is in Christ." Again, we must never rely only on our intellectual minds, but only on the Holy Spirit's guidance.

Our intellect is connected to knowledge, and knowledge can cause us to have pride, as it says in 1 Corinthians 8:1, "Knowledge puffs up, but love edifies." As believers, we do not want to be attached to the tree of the knowledge of good and evil, but to the Tree of Life.

There is something else my wife taught me that can truly apply to every situation in our lives: "We can talk big, but if we do not walk the talk, we are small." We are accountable for what comes out of our mouths.

That was the downfall of most of the Jews in the Holocaust. They believed that since they were God's chosen people, nothing bad would happen to them, and it was only through the hard experience of it that some people came to realize who they really were in their spiritual walk. Unfortunately, that realization came too late for many of the Jews, and they paid for it with their lives.

I pray that if I were in the Holocaust I would have heeded Jabotinsky's words or would have heard the Holy Spirit warning me that danger was coming and that it was time to go back to Israel.

For Christians today, the Holocaust makes us ask ourselves, "If I had been alive during the Holocaust, would I have risked my life to hide the Jews from the Nazis? How much do I really believe that I am grafted into the Olive tree?" (Romans 11:17-18).

Our spiritual walk should be reflected in our physical walk, in how we deal with the world in everyday life. Our faith should be grounded. James 2:14 says, "What does it profit, my brethren, if someone says he has faith but does not have works? Can faith save him?"

That leads me to the next chapter about living by faith in a practical way in our lives.

# Practical Faith

I had a conversation with a secular Jew in Israel about the definition of a Messianic Jew and the meaning of being a Christian. During our conversation, she said she strongly believed in God. I told her that I am a practical person, and so I asked her, "Have you ever made a decision in your life because of God?" She thought about it and honestly said, "No." I replied, "Then, practically speaking, God does not exist for you!"

Many secular Jews say they believe in God, for their peace of mind, for their spiritual security, and so that other people will not think that they are materialistic with no spiritual value. I was like that as well. They live their lives with this attitude of spiritual defense and they believe that doing good things is enough. But is it enough?

As it is said in the book of James 2:24, "You see then that a man is justified by works, and not by faith only." But we are talking about works that reflect your faith, not just good deeds that reflect who you are.

Recently, the Coronavirus caused all of us to take a good look at our "faith" and we got to see how good we really are at keeping our peace and balance in such chaotic days using our faith as a shield and a guide. I would say most of us were made painfully aware that our "faith" was shaken and didn't help us to keep peace and balance.

1 Corinthians 10:13 encourages us believers when it says, "No temptation (ordeal) has overtaken you except such as is common to man; but God is faithful, who will not allow

69

you to be tempted (go through an ordeal) beyond what you are able, but with the temptation (ordeal) will also make the way of escape, that you may be able to bear it."

Again, 2 Corinthians 5:7 says, "For we walk by faith, not by sight." During the Coronavirus we were fighting an enemy that we could not see. This is when we believers should have the upper hand over the non-believers by keeping our composure and adjusting smoothly.

Because we are in the world and not of the world, we should be less attached to whatever our life looked like before the Coronavirus came, provided our walk of faith is solid and practical.

Other people in our lives may have a clearer perception of how grounded our walk of faith is than we do. They can see our flaws better than we can because we are too busy living our lives to see ourselves objectively.

It is like a soccer coach with his players. He can easily see their strengths and weaknesses as he watches from the sidelines, while the players are too close to the action and can't see as clearly how they are really doing. They may think they are fabulous, but they can't see the whole field of play to know how their performance is affecting the game.

We can so easily deceive ourselves into thinking that we are doing great and that it is everyone else that is messing things up. Again, this is why Yeshua said in Matthew 7:3-5, "And why do you look at the speck in your brother's eye, but do not consider the plank in your own eye?... Hypocrite! First remove the plank from your own eye, and then you will see clearly to remove the speck from your brother's eye." We must see clearly first!

My wife puts me on course from time to time in this regard, especially when I am tired and my flesh gives in to the old self. She always reminds me that we must walk in the Spirit and act according to what we preach. She helps me tremendously to have a practical, down-to-earth walk of faith.

It is so important to have someone next to you who loves you enough to share some thoughts of wisdom, like my beloved wife does. I see why the Lord has made us male and female, two beings that can grow together in the physical and in the spirit as well. One leads and one supports, one has the passion, and one has the discipline to maintain that passion, and so on.

"For if they fall, one will lift up his companion. But woe to him who is alone when he falls, for he has no one to help him up. Again, if two lie down together, they will keep warm; but how can one be warm alone?" (Ecclesiastes 4:10-11).

Here's a personal example of applying the word in everyday life that I think most of you will relate to. Driving in Israel can be quite a challenge, and I realize that the stupidity and self-centeredness of the other drivers can pull me right out of the Spirit and into the flesh as I react in like manner and lose my peace. So I have armed myself with a scripture that says, "Why do you not rather accept wrong? Why do you not rather let yourselves be cheated?" (1 Corinthians 6:7).

Reminding myself of this scripture and using self-discipline helps me to have more peace while driving – most of the time! I'm not perfect at it yet – getting there slowly, but surely. I can recite this scripture and then a few seconds later a car cuts me off and my first reaction is anger. My beloved can attest to that!

Still, practice makes perfect, and that's how we need to see it, knowing it will help us to learn better how to be in the world and not of the world!

2 Peter 1:5-7 says, "…giving all diligence, add to your faith virtue, to virtue knowledge, to knowledge self-control, to self-control perseverance, to perseverance godliness, to godliness brotherly kindness, and to brotherly kindness love." The reason it is important to have these virtues is in verse 9. "For he who lacks these things is shortsighted, even to blindness, and has forgotten that he was cleansed from his old sins." We would be blind to His will and would not understand why we are going through an ordeal. And without self-discipline, for example, we could easily become consumed with self-pity and end up behaving like a non-believer despite our faith and love for the Lord.

We see that the disciples themselves had trouble following Yeshua even though they were right there with Him and were given authority and power to heal and cast out demons.

Peter is a good example. When he wanted to walk on water to Yeshua, he couldn't do it because his natural man, the old self, kept him from focusing on the Lord, pulling him from belief to focusing on the storm. His lack of self-control caused him to fail. While he was on the boat, he had the confidence he could do it. But once out of his comfort zone, he saw where his faith really was when he tried to walk on the water to Yeshua.

And even though he had said he was willing to die for Yeshua, he wound up denying Him three times because fear took over and he acted like a non-believer, as we see in Matthew 26:69-75. But despite all his failures, the Lord still asked him to feed His sheep in John 21:17. Because He knew it was only a matter of time before Peter would be mature enough to lead the disciples.

Peter was willing, and that is what we need to remember. We are not perfect, either, but we need to have the tenacity to continue despite our imperfections and mistakes.

In the Garden of Gethsemane, when Yeshua's soul was exceedingly sorrowful, even to death, He told the disciples to stay and watch with Him. When He came back and found them sleeping when He needed them the most, He said to them, "Watch and pray, lest you enter into temptation. The spirit indeed is willing, but the flesh is weak." (Matthew 26:41).

The influence of our body on us is strong, and it also affects our spiritual walk, especially when we are tired, as I mentioned before. I learned that early on. My workouts would make me so exhausted that it weakened my walk of faith. I would give in to the exhaustion and wasn't as alert in the Spirit as I needed to be. The Lord really taught me that I needed to be balanced in that area.

In our walk of faith, even when we make mistakes, the Lord can turn it for our benefit if our hearts are right and we are truly seeking and following Him. I have said this before, but it bears repeating. The English translation of Genesis 17:1 says, "Walk before Me and be blameless," but in Hebrew it says, "Walk before Me and be innocent." That is a completely different meaning! He is not telling us to be perfect, but to be innocent as a child who wants to please his father but who sometimes makes mistakes. He wants us to be close to Him.

I came to realize that the Lord uses the physical world with its relationships and circumstances to teach us to modify and solidify our walk of faith. That is the practical aspect of faith. But for us to apply it in everyday life, we need to be detached and to discipline our thoughts.

Hebrews 12:7-8 shows us another aspect of discipline. "If you endure chastening ("suffer" in Hebrew), God deals with you as with sons; for what son is there whom a father does not chasten? But if you are without chastening, of which all have become partakers, then you are illegitimate and not sons." He does it for our benefit that we may be partakers of His holiness. It's not fun at the time, but the fruit will come later on.

Yeshua knows that if we discipline our thoughts, it will help us to discipline our actions. "But I say to you that whoever looks at a woman to lust for her has already committed adultery with her in his heart" (Matthew 5:28). We must have self-control in order to act as a believer!!! And it starts with control over our thoughts.

Again, the Lord said in Genesis 4:7, "Whether you do well or not, sin lies at the door, and you have a desire to it, but you will rule over it" (Hebrew translation). We can control ourselves so we will not sin.

There is another pitfall to our practical walk of faith that can happen even to believers who are devoted and focused on doing things for the Lord, who are willing to suffer and have suffered for His name, and who have patience and endurance. That pitfall is doing things out of habit and losing passion and love for the Lord.

This happened at the church of Ephesus. Yeshua told them in Revelation 2:4, "Nevertheless, I have this against you, that you have left your first love."

The way out of such a situation is shown in Revelation 2:5, "Remember therefore from where you have fallen; repent and do the first works…"

It is like renewing the fire in your love relationship with your wife. Habits and the pressures of life easily put a burden on you, and you lose the passion you had in the beginning of your relationship.

In order to avoid bad habits and automatic behavior, Yeshua told His disciples in Luke 10:7, "Do not go from house to house." When spreading the gospel, if you find a house that receives you, stay there. Be tuned in to the Holy Spirit and don't just knock on every door so that at the end of the day you can pat yourself on the back and put notches in your belt.

Another pitfall in our walk of faith can be when we focus on knowing, learning, and understanding the word but not on living by the word. James 2:17 says, "Thus also faith by itself, if it does not have works, is dead."

The focus must be on Him for your spiritual peace and security, not on you and your activities. We need to remember the instruction in Proverbs 3:6, "In all your ways acknowledge Him, and He shall direct your paths."

Just as important as having faith is keeping the faith. Yeshua said in Luke 11:28, "…blessed are those who hear the word of God and keep it." The word of God is essential to our walk of faith. The Hebrew word for "keep" also means "guard."

Yeshua taught many truths in the parable of the seeds in Matthew 13:19-23. If someone does not understand the word of the kingdom, then the wicked one comes and snatches away what was sown in his heart. One who receives the word happily yet has no root in himself endures only for a while. Some immediately stumble when trouble or persecution comes. Others become unfruitful when the cares of the world or deceitfulness of riches choke the word.

We must guard our faith from the pressures of the world and from Satan who is out there trying to stop the believers.

In addition to the everyday challenges we face in life, we have been confronted these days with more and more hardships, such as the Coronavirus and loss of jobs, which Yeshua told us would happen. He said in Matthew 18:7, "Woe to the world because of offenses (obstacles)! For offenses must come…".

Yeshua also prophesied about the destruction of Jerusalem and the Holy Temple and gave His disciples practical advice in Luke 21:20-21, "But when you see Jerusalem surrounded by armies, then know that its desolation is near. Then let those who are in Judea flee to the mountains, let those who are in the midst of her depart, and let not those who are in the country enter her."

Prophecy is a very practical tool for the future in our walk of faith. It teaches us how to respond when tribulations come, and I think we can all agree that they have already started. Our lives may depend on how we respond to prophecy being fulfilled.

Romans 5:3-4 says, "…we also glory in tribulations, knowing that tribulation produces perseverance; and perseverance, character; and character, hope." I try to see the hardships we go through in that light, and I ask the Lord why certain things have happened and what He wants me to do.

Knowing the word of God gives us hope for our lives now and beyond this world. "Hope" in Hebrew is "tikva" and the root of the word is "kav" which means "line." The last letter is "Hay," which I mentioned before represents God, so the word "hope" means a line to or with God.

We see the purpose of having tribulations. And with discipline, we can even rejoice when harder times come instead of getting caught in self-pity.

In Philippians 1:29 it says that we are "...not only to believe in Him, but also to suffer for His sake..." Are we willing to do that?

Ecclesiastes 9:2 reminds us that "One event happens to the righteous and the wicked...". Good and bad things happen to everyone. We cannot avoid the hard times, but we need to endure them, as Yeshua told us in Matthew 24:13. "But He who endures to the end shall be saved."

He lets us know about the hard times to come in advance through prophecy, and shows us how to take steps accordingly, being guided by the Holy Spirit to make the changes needed to adjust to the new circumstances. Hard times can build us, build our faith, and build our self-confidence in our walk of faith.

A good example of this is King David. Long before he was king, David was able to face Goliath because he had already faced a lion and a bear while protecting his sheep. Knowing that it was the Lord who had helped him, he was able to say boldly, "The Lord, who delivered me from the paw of the lion and from the paw of the bear, He will deliver me from the hand of this Philistine." (1 Samuel 17:37).

Later, when he was king and again faced tremendous threats and obstacles, David was able to encourage himself in the Lord as he remembered the faithfulness of God.

The same goes for us. We can encourage ourselves in the Lord as we remember how the Lord has helped us thus far and know that He will never leave us or forsake us. That is also where the power of our testimony comes in. Revelation 12:11 says, "And they overcame him by the blood of the Lamb and by the word of their testimony, and they did not love their lives to the death."

Another pitfall for believers in our walk of faith is expecting something in return, such as prosperity, success, etc. When that does not happen, many fall out of faith.

It happens today as it happened to those who have gone before us. Malachi 3:14 showed us how the people complained harshly. "You have said, 'It is useless to serve God; What profit is it that we have kept His ordinance…?'"

Then there is also the opposite example of people the Lord had helped to prosper who were then hit with hard times and lost much. It can affect your walk of faith as you ask yourself, "Where is God?" This is exactly what the Jews asked during the Holocaust.

Through Yeshua we learn to love selflessly, without expectation or demands, and that is why Yeshua tells us to love our enemies and to love those who don't love us. "For if you love those who love you, what reward have you? Do not even the tax collectors do the same?" (Matthew 5:46).

Loving your enemies helps you to be able to deny yourself. Not to focus on your own feelings so that, as the scripture says, we can follow Yeshua.

The story in the book of Job shows us that the Lord also uses Satan to test our faith. In Job 1:9, Satan answered the Lord regarding Job's faith, saying, "Does Job fear (respect) God for nothing?" And in verse 10, he said, "You have blessed the work of his hands, and his possessions have increased in the land." That is why Satan made a plan to take away all that Job had to prove that it would affect his faith. As we see in Job 1:11, "But now, stretch out Your hand and touch all that he has, and he will surely curse You to Your face!"

Our true and practical walk of faith should not be connected to or affected by how much we possess, and that is expressed in Job's reaction in verse 21. "The Lord gave, and the Lord has taken away; Blessed be the name of the Lord." We are talking also of the loss of his sons and daughters, not only of his possessions.

To be able to have this kind of attitude when calamity hits, we must first have this kind of attitude when things are going well.

Again, 1 Corinthians 7:29-36 describes, in a very practical way, how to be in the world and not of the world. The reasons for it are in verse 29, "...the time is short..." and in verse 32, "But I want you to be without care." And the purpose for it is in verse 35, "...that you may serve the Lord without distraction." The world and its affairs can easily distract us believers, as we learned well during the Coronavirus.

We need to think of it the way we would think of a father teaching his children about life, telling them what to do and what not to do. For example, he would tell them not to touch a hot pan or they would get burned.

I give the example of a father's love because the word "love" in Hebrew is "ahava." You can see the letter "Hay" that represents the Lord and then "av" which means "father." The Father's love is the true and real love, and I believe that is the reason you can find Him in the word "love" in Hebrew.

If we do not obey, then we get burned, and we learn the hard way that it is better to obey the Father than to stubbornly hold on to our own ways and what we are used to, such as tradition.

# Tradition and the Return to Israel

We have all heard the phrase, "Carrying on the family tradition!" This can be a son following in his father's footsteps as he takes over the business his father worked all his life to build, or it can be celebrating holidays in ways that you grew up with, or cooking foods that were great-grandma's favorite recipes. Basically, it's observing ways of doing things that have gone on for generations.

Tradition gives us security. The examples above give us physical and family security. This is fine, but it can distract us and sometimes even override our need for spiritual security. Everyone who really believes in God needs to seek spiritual security and not family security.

Unfortunately, most of us try to do this by perfecting the laws of tradition, thinking it will give us spiritual security. But it causes us to focus on ourselves and our works instead of focusing on Him, and that does not give us real spiritual security.

Tradition should be like the frame to the picture, to keep it together like it kept the Jewish people together in exile, but for them it wound up becoming the picture itself.

We all need spiritual security, and it manifests in our lives in various ways, depending on our walk with the Lord. The most common way is through tradition, but there is a pitfall here because tradition causes us to be self- focused and stops us from having a relationship with the Lord.

Tradition also keeps us in the same place without any renewal of our minds. I mentioned before that in

Romans 12:2 it says, "…be transformed by the renewing of your mind, that you may prove (discern) what is that good and acceptable and perfect will of God."

If we don't renew our minds but just keep doing what we've always done and acting in ways we have always acted, then we will not discern His will and end up deceiving ourselves, thinking that we are following Him.

If the Jews in Europe before the Holocaust had discerned that the time of exile had ended and that the Lord was wanting them to go back to Israel, then it is very possible that the Holocaust would not have happened.

Self-focus results in blocking out the world around you, as I mentioned in the chapter about the horse with blinders. Focusing on yourself and meticulously keeping the traditions that fortify your idea of faith can give you a false sense of security.

The danger in it is that you become blind to reality, and you will not be able to see what is coming at you from the people around you until it is too late. That is one of the reasons for what happened in the Holocaust.

Many Christians have been going the same way as the Jews, putting tradition and customs first. Going to church every Sunday does not make you a Christian. I compare going to church with going to the gym. When you are in the gym, you get puffed up, you use your muscles more intensely than you do on other days. The same thing happens when you go to church; you feel elated, spiritual, closer to God than during the week. We know that the Lord wants us to worship, but it is for Him.

After working out, if we don't get the right nutrition and rest, our muscles will not grow. It is the same with our spiritual life. If we don't apply the word during the week, we don't grow in our faith. James 2:22 says, "Do you see that faith was working together with his works, and by works faith was made perfect?"

When tradition is the main thing in our lives, then the concerns of this life will choke our faith, as Yeshua said in the parable of the seeds. Matthew 13:22 says, "Now he who received seed among the thorns is he who hears the word, and the cares of this world and the deceitfulness of riches choke the word, and he becomes unfruitful."

We see that the real focus of the Jews since the destruction of the second temple has been to survive and to keep the people united. For their spiritual adjustment and security, there was a need to write the oral law and to study that more than the Bible. The focus was on the people and their needs and not on God and His will. Therefore, the rabbis became the spiritual leaders, and everything was conducted by and through them.

We showed when this really began, in 1 Samuel 8:7. "And the Lord said to Samuel, 'Heed the voice of the people in all that they say to you; for they have not rejected you, but they have rejected Me, that I should not reign over them.'" The people of Israel wanted to be like the rest of the nations who had kings and wanted to follow a human being instead of following God.

Yeshua asked in Matthew 15:3, "Why do you also transgress the commandment of God because of your tradition?"

Tradition helps you to feel good about yourself spiritually, but it also blinds you from the truth of your walk of faith.

Take Passover, for example. The Jews are so happy with what the Lord did for us by getting us out of Egypt, out of slavery to freedom, and so on. But we don't talk about what happened after they crossed the red sea, as if the story ended there. We don't talk about the fact that all the people who came out of Egypt who were 20 years old and up died in the desert, including Moses and Aaron, the leaders (except for Joshua and Caleb).

The purpose of the Exodus was for them to come to Israel and have a country for themselves. In that regard, the Exodus was not successful for most of them.

"Therefore, behold, the days are coming," says the Lord, "that they shall no longer say, 'As the Lord lives who brought up the children of Israel from the land of Egypt,' but, 'As the Lord lives who brought up and led the descendants of the house of Israel from the north country and from all the countries where I had driven them.' And they shall dwell in their own land." (Jeremiah 23:7-8).

He is saying they should no longer be focusing on the Exodus from Egypt, but on the Exodus from exile to Israel that has been happening since the Holocaust. If we focus on that and how important it is to the Lord, then many Jews who now live all around the world would not have peace while still living in exile. But when you focus on tradition, you don't face that. You don't face His will, His words.

As a conclusion to this chapter, I want to clarify something. I know that I have written pretty harshly against tradition, but it does not mean that I am saying we need to eradicate it from our walk of faith. I am saying to not let tradition overshadow our walk and become the main factor.

For example, we need to celebrate Passover, but not necessarily the way it has been done up to now, reading the Haggadah as the main part of our celebration, as it is a product of the oral law, not God's commandment. We should not be rigid in our traditional activities, but see the whole picture, focusing on His will and His way and not the rabbis' way.

We can see what happened to the Jews when they did not follow the Lord's commandments nor listen to the prophets He had sent to tell them His will.

One chapter in Deuteronomy gives us an especially vivid description of the Holocaust and what happens when we don't follow His will.

# Deuteronomy Chapter 28

While reading Chapter 28 of Deuteronomy, I suddenly realized that I was reading the description of the Holocaust. The chapter begins with the blessings we receive from God if we obey Him. But then comes the rest of the chapter that describes what will happen if we do not obey Him and His commandments.

"But it shall come to pass, if you do not obey the voice of the Lord your God, to observe carefully all His commandments and His statutes which I command you today, that all these curses will come upon you…" (verse 15).

The description of the Holocaust starts in verse 22, "…they shall pursue you until you perish." The Nazis' plan was to exterminate the Jews. Then in verse 25, "…you shall become troublesome to all the kingdoms of the earth."

No country at that time wanted to keep the Jews, not even the United States. And the British made every effort to stop the Jews from coming to Israel, even though it was the British who helped defeat Germany. What a strange contradiction. In verse 29 it says, "…you shall be only oppressed and plundered continually, and no one shall save you." No nation came to help the Jews.

Verse 26 says, "Your carcasses shall be food for all the birds of the air and the beasts of the earth…" We saw the dead bodies with no graves in the concentration camps.

Verse 34 summarizes it all, "So you shall be driven mad because of the sight which your eyes see." To this day, we cannot overcome the sight of the dead bodies that were found in the concentration camps. Skin and bones because of starvation, and naked because the Germans took everything they had.

It also describes the situation in Germany before the Holocaust in verse 43 where it says, "The alien who is among you shall rise higher and higher above you, and you shall come down lower and lower."

The status of the Jews in Germany dropped lower and lower as the status of the Nazis climbed higher and higher. The Germans took the Jews' assets step by step until they had nothing.

Hitler wanted to destroy the Jews as in verse 45, "Moreover all these curses shall come upon you and pursue and overtake you, until you are destroyed..."

And in verse 48, "...you shall serve your enemies, whom the Lord will send against you, in hunger, in thirst, in nakedness, and in need of everything; and He will put a yoke of iron on your neck until He has destroyed you." Doesn't this describe the Jews working for the Germans in the concentration camps?

Verses 52-58 describe the extreme hunger that the Jews would have and how they would really suffer during the Holocaust. Verses 64-65, "Then the Lord will scatter you among all peoples, from one end of the earth to the other, and there you shall serve other gods, which neither you nor your fathers have known – wood and stone. And among those nations you shall find no rest..."

The Jews have been in exile for 2,000 years and they have had to move from place to place because of persecution. They have been called "The Nomad Jew." How correct that is.

Verses 66-67 speak of the fear the Jews would have. "Your life shall hang in doubt before you; you shall fear day and night, and have no assurance of life." Such was the situation of the Jews during the Holocaust. "…because of the fear which terrifies your heart, and because of the sight which your eyes see."

This chapter describes both the Holocaust and the exile of the Jews to the world, and the reason for it, as stated in verse 62 where it says, "You shall be left few in number…because you would not obey the voice of the Lord your God."

In verse 47 it says, "Because you did not serve the Lord your God with joy and gladness of heart, for the abundance of everything…"

History has repeated itself again and again throughout the Bible, and whenever Israel did not walk according to His will, they suffered. It is only logical and spiritual to presume that this situation also continues after the time of the Bible. If we do not believe that, then we are cut off from our roots, from Israel, and from God – the Lord of Abraham, Isaac, and Jacob.

It is a crucial point to understand and to be clear about so that we have a starting point to fathom the Lord's will in the Holocaust.

We all go through temptations in life, and most of us fall prey to the temptation of possessing the things of the world. But, interestingly, the Jews, before the Holocaust, were attempting to prove to the Lord and to the world that they were the chosen people.

# Deuteronomy Chapter 28

When Yeshua was tested by Satan, He was tested to prove that He was the Son of God by showing His power: "If You are the Son of God, command that these stones to become bread," and by testing the Father's will regarding Himself: "If You are the Son of God, throw Yourself down (from the highest point of the Temple). For it is written: 'He shall give His angels charge over you … In their hands they shall bear you up, lest you dash your foot against a stone.'" The third test was to tempt Yeshua with the kingdoms of the world: "All these things I will give You if You fall down and worship me."

That was the pitfall of the Jews; they were sure that they knew the Lord and that He would protect them, no matter what. That is why the Jews needed to be different from other people. They are not focused on the same temptation as most people, on the surface.

We see the description of the Holocaust in Deuteronomy 28, and the word "holocaust" in the Hebrew translation appears in the Bible at least three times. The word "holocaust" does not appear in the English translation of the Bible.

Zephaniah 1:15 says, "That day is a day of wrath, a day of trouble and distress, a day of devastation and desolation, a day of darkness and gloominess, a day of clouds and thick darkness…"

What a description of the day of judgement of the Lord, so no wonder in Hebrew the word for holocaust is used, and that is "shoa." Usually, we spell it "shoah," but here it is spelled such that if we read it the opposite way, from left to right, it is the Hebrew word "ha-esh" which means the fire, "His fire."

The Holocaust is actually "His fire" that consumed the Jews in Europe. Hebrews 12:29 says, "For our God is a consuming fire." And Isaiah 66:16 says, "For by fire and by His sword the Lord will judge all flesh…"

Then in Isaiah 10:3, the word "holocaust" appears in Hebrew. In Hebrew, "desolation" and "holocaust" are the same word, "shoah." It says, "What will you do in the day of punishment, and in the desolation which will come from afar? To whom will you flee for help? And where will you leave your glory (your pride, respect, in Hebrew)?"

We have the same issue in the Holocaust. Who helped the Jews to escape from the Nazis? And the humiliation that the Jews had suffered during and even before the Holocaust (as things had already become unbearable for the Jews in Germany and Austria since 1938)?

Then in Ezekiel 38:9, the Lord describes Gog, the prince of Rosh, coming against Israel. "You will ascend, coming like a storm (holocaust), covering the land like a cloud, you and all your troops and many peoples with you."

A description of the Nazis covering Europe, coming fast like a storm. In Germany, there was a unit called the storm troopers, who were known for their aggressiveness, violence, and brutality in both World Wars.

You see how the use of the word holocaust (shoa) in the Bible shows us things about the Holocaust in Europe. It is because of His will, His plan for His people Israel. And Ezekiel 37:1-14, the vision and prophecy of the dry bones, describes the piles of starved, dead bodies in the concentration camps. Yet out of the Holocaust the nation of Israel was born!!!

# Deuteronomy Chapter 28

The Lord's will, the fear of the Lord, and the Lord's justice are subjects that I am going to elaborate on for us to better understand the Holocaust.

# The Lord's Will

Several years ago, my beloved wife and I needed to quickly find a new place to live in the Jerusalem area. We found a place we liked but could not move into right away since the current tenants had six months left on their lease. Meaning, we would have to find another place to live for six months and then move into our new home.

I was sure that the place was not the one God had for us since I believed He would not make us move twice. I believed that if it was His will, things would go smoothly! Therefore, even though the place was great, I gave my beloved quite a hard time before finally accepting the fact that it was the one for us.

The smooth way is not always the way that He chooses for us, since we can learn a lot along the way. And actually, "the way" is more important than the destination. Yeshua said, "I am the way, the truth, and the life." But to us, the destination seems more important, although that may not necessarily be His will or His plan. 2 Timothy 1:9 shows us that God "…called us with a holy calling, not according to our works, but according to His own purpose…"

It was on our way to see the new place again when the Lord gave me a revelation. I had been stubborn and so sure that I knew the will of God, just as many Jews in Europe before the Holocaust were convinced that the Lord would protect them since they did everything to show they were His chosen people.

The Lord's Will

It was, and still is, hard for most Jews to change their ways. As Jeremiah said in Jeremiah 13:22, "Can the Ethiopian change his skin or the leopard its spots?" So there was, and still is, a resistance to accept His will, His way.

When the Jews were told to surrender Jerusalem to the Chaldeans, they were not willing to do that, which meant that they did not really believe in God and instead focused on their actions of sacrifices in the Holy Temple as they had done for many years. Their own thinking and feelings came first and caused them to decide to stay and fight.

The Jews could not understand the ways of God when Jeremiah told them to surrender to the Chaldeans, so they refused to listen to Jeremiah. It did not fit their sense of pride to become slaves, nor their patriotism for Jerusalem and the Holy Temple. It would be that way today, too. It would require a strong walk of faith to surrender and not fight.

Many times in the Bible we see that the will and the ways of God do not follow normal human logic. 1 Samuel 15:3 says, "Now go and attack Amalek, and utterly destroy all that they have, and do not spare them. But kill both man and woman, infant and nursing child, ox and sheep, camel and donkey."

Saul, of course, could not let all the good spoil be killed, and he captured the king and spared all the choice livestock, as any normal person in his right mind would do. When confronted by Samuel, he tried to justify it by saying they were going to sacrifice them to the Lord.

Samuel told him in 1 Samuel 15:22, "Behold, to obey is better than sacrifice…" and said in verse 23, "Because you have rejected the word of the Lord, He also has rejected you from being king." In verse 24, Saul replied, "…I feared the people and obeyed their voice."

Our natural tendency is to fear people more than God since they are visible, and their words and actions affect us directly. But that disobedience was the beginning of the end for Saul.

To obey God puts the focus on Him, while sacrifice puts the focus on us. "For I desire mercy and not sacrifice, and the knowledge of God more than burnt offerings." (Hosea 6:6).

Obedience to God can sometimes make us feel uncertain, unsure. It requires that we can't rely on our own reasoning and that we must let go of the control of our lives to Him. It also requires patience, as we must also wait for His timing, which 99 percent of the time is not our timing! This can be very scary for us, since from birth we learn how to control people, circumstances, our actions, etc.

To obey Him, we must sacrifice of ourselves, not animals. That was a new concept for the people of Israel, who until Samuel, believed all could be taken care of with sacrifices of animals to the Lord.

It is much harder to obey Him personally than it is to sacrifice animals to Him, believing that that act alone will put us back on track with the Lord with no further efforts on our part.

The Lord's will cannot be understood by using man's wisdom because He sees the whole picture, including the future, while we do not, and we rely on our minds to set the course of our lives by what we see now in the present.

That is why most Jews rely on acting according to tradition rather than focusing on living according to His will.

The Lord's Will

Living according to His will requires denying yourself and following Him. Again, the scripture in Psalm 46:10, "Be still ("let go" in Hebrew) and know that I am God" tells us that, as well. When we let Him control our lives by letting go of our control, then we will see and know God.

Job believed we should accept the Lord's will, as he said in Job 2:10, "Shall we indeed accept good from God, and shall we not accept adversity?" It is hard for us to accept that the Lord who loves us would also let us go through extremely hard times. It just doesn't make sense to us. But if we imagine a father that sometimes spanks his kids when they are not obeying him, then we can understand God sometimes brings hard times upon us. Many times, it is the consequences of our actions and not "just" the Lord testing us.

There were many innocent Jewish people who died in the Holocaust, but they did not know the Lord's will and did not understand that it was time to come back to Israel (the end of their exile), which grieves me to this day. It was their leaders, their rabbis, for example, who did not discern that it was time to come back to Israel, and their followers suffered because of them.

We saw another example of how we suffered because of our leaders in 1 Kings 20:42. "Thus says the Lord: 'Because you (Ahab, the king of Israel) have let slip out of your hand a man whom I appointed to utter destruction, therefore your life shall go for his life, and your people for his people.'"

Not following His will makes you no different from a non-believer whom the Lord rejects. "Not everyone who says to Me, 'Lord, Lord,' shall enter the kingdom of heaven, but he who does the will of My Father in heaven. Many will say to Me in that day, 'Lord, Lord, have we not prophesied in Your name, cast out demons in Your name, and done many wonders in Your name?' And then I will declare to them, 'I never knew you; depart from Me, you who practice lawlessness!'" (Matthew 7:21-23).

So, it is not only tradition that can cause us to deceive ourselves, but also lack of knowledge of the Lord and knowing His will. Just as King Saul had lost his kingdom, Israel had lost its kingdom and was sent into exile. "Your burnt offerings are not acceptable, nor your sacrifices sweet to Me." (Jeremiah 6:20).

We can sacrifice as many bulls and goats as possible, but if we don't obey Him and walk according to His will, then it's useless. And if we compare sacrifice to tradition, we see that keeping the traditions as strictly as possible did not save the Jews from the Holocaust. But did the Jews make any changes in this regard after the Holocaust?

The Promised Land that was given to the Jews by God in the time of Joshua, and the Holy Temple built by the great King Solomon, were destroyed and the Jews sent into exile. What devastation to all that the Jews had believed in!

Another aspect of the Lord's will can be described in Jeremiah chapter 18:6, "O house of Israel, can I not do with you as this potter?" says the Lord. "Look, as the clay is in the potter's hand, so are you in My hand, O house of Israel!"

The Lord here simply expresses His desire to mold us as a nation and as individuals. We need to allow Him to mold each of our lives into the shape He desires. But how can He shape us if we insist on following our own will, our own way?

# The Lord's Will

The people of Israel had to be broken and suffer at times throughout history, and then they cried out to the Lord. We can see that again and again in the Book of Judges.

To summarize, the Lord shows us in the Bible that He desires us to obey Him and to be willing to be molded by Him. He also desires for us to fear Him as He said in Jeremiah 2:19, "...and the fear of Me is not in you..." and because of that the people of Israel had forsaken Him. I will elaborate on fearing the Lord in the next chapter.

Sometimes my people have had too much confidence in themselves because they were called to be the chosen ones and thought they could do whatever they wished even it was outside of God's ways. This is the false security they've had in themselves and in the Holy Temple. This is not what God intended.

"For you are a holy people to the Lord your God; the Lord your God has chosen you to be a people for Himself, a special treasure above all the peoples on the face of the earth. The Lord did not set His love on you nor choose you because you were more in number than any other people, for you were the least of all peoples; but because the Lord loves you, and because He would keep the oath which He swore to your fathers, the Lord has brought you out with a mighty hand, and redeemed you from the house of bondage, from the hand of Pharaoh king of Egypt." (Deuteronomy 7:6-8).

We are to be a light to the world, but it is only possible if we follow His will. And if we don't, then the scripture in Isaiah 10:17 tells us what happens to that light, "So the Light of Israel will be for a fire, and his Holy One for a flame; it will burn and devour..."

For example, the Lord explains why His people were sent into exile in Jeremiah 5:19. "And it will be when you say, 'Why does the Lord our God do all these things to us?' then you shall answer them, 'Just as you have forsaken Me and served foreign gods in your land, so you shall serve aliens in a land that is not yours.'" The scripture shows with clarity His will and His actions.

Thankfully, through Yeshua, we can discern and know His will. "And we have such trust through Christ (The Messiah) toward God." (2 Corinthians 3:4).

But not knowing His will and not knowing Him leads me to another point I want to talk about. The lack of the fear of the Lord.

# The Fear of the Lord

In Jeremiah 32:38-39, the Lord says, after bringing His people back to Israel, "They shall be My people, and I will be their God; then I will give them one heart and one way, that that they may fear Me forever..."

God does not want us to fear Him because of what He might do to us, but because He does not want us to take Him for granted as though He were just a bystander in our lives.

The Hebrew word that is used here, "yir'ah," means "fear out of respect," and the root of the word is "ra'ah" which means "to see." It is the fear that comes from respecting the Lord as we see His works. Fear is an important factor in our faith that comes from knowing the Lord and respecting Him. If we don't see His works, then we also won't fear Him.

Unfortunately, in the Middle Ages, the church used fear and the threat of hell and destruction to those who would not come to church.

But if you don't truly know Him, then you don't fear (respect) Him, because you are not afraid of someone you don't know and can't see.

For example, if you're sitting next to a man on a train and don't know that he is a cruel killer, you don't fear him. But if you recognize him from a police photo you had seen on TV, then you would most likely be shaking in your boots and trying to get as far away from him as you possibly could. Fear that comes from recognition is what I mean here. Only it is the Lord we are talking about, as in Job 23:14 when it says, "Therefore I am terrified at His presence…"

The problem is that we only see the results of His actions and don't see Him directly. It is like seeing trees moving by the wind, but you can't see the wind. That is why knowing Him and discerning His actions in our lives and in the world is crucial. It is what gives us a healthy fear of the Lord. "The Fear of the Lord is the beginning of wisdom, and the knowledge of the Holy One is understanding." (Proverbs 9:10).

If we imagine ourselves as children who love their father, will that love really be enough for us to obey him? No, because our selfishness and curiosity come first, so chances are we will not obey all of our father's commandments. But if we fear him as well, the chances are better that we will obey him.

Unfortunately, our flesh – our feelings and desires – cause most of us to put ourselves first, even if we say we are trying to follow His commandments. The result is that most of us do not follow Him, but instead follow our own way. But if we fear the Lord – fear that comes from respect for Him – then we would think twice before going our own way.

In Hosea 4:6, God says, "My people are destroyed for lack of knowledge. Because you have rejected knowledge (of the Lord), I also will reject you from being priest for Me; because you have forgotten the law of your God, I also will forget your children."

The Lord is saying here that not knowing Him, not knowing His will, would bring disaster to His people.

Many Jews in Europe during the Second World War did not know God. They did not see that He wanted them to come back to Israel, and so disaster came upon them as it is written here in Hosea. How necessary it is to always seek the Lord!

I will mention again Hosea 6:6 as a reminder of how important it is to the Lord that His people would know Him. "For I desire mercy and not sacrifice, and the knowledge of God more than burnt offerings." The Lord wants us "to know" Him more than he wants us "to do" for Him. The Jews thought that burnt offerings were "the thing to do" in order to have peace with the Lord.

The religious Jews have tried, through knowledge of the verbal law – the Mishna, the Gemara, the Talmud, etc. – to build a spiritual way. It doesn't work, because it is not based on knowing God, but rather on knowing the wisdom of men.

If we follow Him and keep the first commandment to "...love the Lord your God with all your heart, with all your soul, with all your mind, with all your strength," then we will be more focused on knowing Him and His will regarding our actions.

One day, while driving to work in Jerusalem, I picked up a religious Jew who was needing a ride. I asked him where he was going, and he said he was going to visit the site of Rachel's Tomb. I asked him if he thought the Lord wanted him to go there. He said it was for himself that he was going there.

Then I said, "Aren't we supposed to put Him first and consider whether He is happy with our actions rather than just doing things for ourselves?" He could not answer me clearly.

There is the problem. We need to think about how the Lord views the things that we do and consider whether they are in line with His will and priorities in our lives and if it is something that He wants us to do.

There are so many false prophets among us today, and one reason for this is the lack of the fear of God. People can wind up giving a prophecy they think is from God, but God did not put those words in their mouths.

And what is not of God is of Satan, as Yeshua told Peter in Matthew 16:23, "Get behind Me, Satan! You are an offense to Me, for you are not mindful of the things of God, but the things of men."

As I said earlier, Peter had expressed himself in a very human way, as I think most of us would if we had heard that our loved one was going to be tortured and crucified. But this is when we need to go beyond our own feelings and put Him and His will (His plan) first.

As I said before, denying ourselves is crucial in order to follow Him and not our own feelings, no matter how human and compassionate those feelings are.

Keeping the faith is the most difficult when hard times befall us or our loved ones. The Jews during the Holocaust thought God was so far away from their lives then, and many chose not to be identified as Jews but as fellow countrymen of the people they were living among. They just wanted to live in peace like everyone else. Many became so comfortable with their way of life that they ignored the warning signs and adapted to the subtle changes that were happening, and that eventually led to their destruction. We ourselves can be the same way, not even discerning that our walk with the Lord might be getting weaker.

Isaiah 29:13 says, "Inasmuch as these people draw near with their mouths and honor Me with their lips, but have removed their hearts far from Me, and their fear toward Me is taught by the commandment of men..." True fear of God was not really there.

Years ago, after the Sandy Hook school shooting took place in the United States, one of the headlines on TV was, "Finding faith in dark times." It caught my eye and made me realize that if we need to "find" faith, it must mean that it isn't already there. But it is only when hard times come that we realize we don't have faith and need to make efforts to find it, even if we thought we had faith before a crisis hit.

It was the same for the Jews during the Holocaust; they had lost faith in God as they were persecuted, gathered in ghettos, taken like cattle to concentration camps, etc. When security disappears, we need to examine our own hearts to see what we really rely on for security. Is it our surroundings, our money, the government, or the Lord?

This is exactly what happened during the Coronavirus. Changes were suddenly mandated by the government to stop the spread of the virus. Changes that affected all of us in many areas of our lives. If we relied on the government and were not prepared, then anger, depression, and frustration hit us.

It is during hard or dark times that we can see very clearly where we are in our walk of faith if we are not too overwhelmed with the physical issues of life.

Satan knows that, and that is why he told the Lord that Job only believed in God because he was in good health and had so many possessions. He said that if everything would be taken from Job, then the Lord would see that he had no faith at all, as described in Job chapter 1.

Again, Jeremiah 9:6 says, "Through deceit they refuse to know Me, says the Lord." Not only can we deceive ourselves, but it is hard for us to receive correction due to pride and stubbornness. Even in our sufferings, we don't always see where we are, and we turn our backs to the Lord. Jeremiah 5:3 says, "You have consumed them, but they have refused to receive correction."

We need to remember that the Lord does not let us experience more than we can handle. 2 Corinthians 4 tells us we may be pressed, but we are not crushed. We may be struck down, but we are not destroyed. This is, of course, if we are believers.

We are to rejoice in tribulations and not get to the point where we are having to "find" faith in dark times, as the TV reporter had said.

Romans 5:3-4 tells us that tribulation produces perseverance, character, and hope. Again, this is provided we have discipline and patience as well as faith, as we see in 2 Peter 1:5-6. I know I have quoted this several times, but it is crucial to our walk. Otherwise, despite our faith, we may become blind to discern His will and will not have the patience to wait on the Lord, especially in dark times.

Last word: we need to remember the Holocaust. We need to understand the fear of the Lord and remember how important it is to hear Him. When the Holy Spirit guides you, then another calamity can be avoided. Not because we have a country and a strong army.

# The Fear of the Lord

A Jewish man once told me, "There is more in Judaism than you know, and you are missing that." There is, but that knowledge will not be helpful or edifying. "...all things are lawful for me, but not all things edify." (1 Corinthians 10:23). What I and all believers need is a relationship with the Lord and to hear the Holy Spirit's guidance.

When your faith is based on knowledge of the verbal law alone, then there is no fear of God that is based on relationship and closeness.

I shared in the first chapter how the Lord showed me to move to the northern part of Israel before the Coronavirus had spread outside of China. It turned out to be the best thing for us. I did not know that the coming change would affect everyone on the planet. I thought it would be something personal that would occur and that's why we needed to move to the north.

When we did move, it was like going from a prison to a resort, with a beautiful view of the Kinneret (the Sea of Galilee). It was less crowded, and it was so much easier for us during the Coronavirus lockdowns.

That is an example of how faith can help you in a practical way during a difficult time, and you don't need to "find" faith or "find" Him, because He has always been there with you in your walk!

Persecution of the Jews in Europe before and during the Holocaust continues to this day, and that is why it is so critical that we hear the voice of the Lord.

# Hunting For the Jews – Destination Israel

The Lord informs Jeremiah in chapter 16 about restoring His people and bringing them back to His land that He had given to their forefathers for them to dwell in. In verse 16, He says, "Behold, I will send for many fishermen," says the Lord, "and they shall fish them; and afterward, I will send for many hunters, and they shall hunt them from every mountain and every hill, and out of the holes of the rocks."

Again, He is saying it is best for Jews to be fished out of the countries that they have found to be pleasant, because after the fishermen, the hunters will come and find them and hunt them down for their demise.

When the hunters come, they will be hunted down, just like what happened in the Holocaust. It is so plain to understand that the Lord wants His people to return home in safety before they are hunted. When you are hunted, you will be wounded or killed.

This title, "Hunting for Jews" was on a U.S TV broadcast in mid-May, 2021, when pro-Palestinian young men were going through the streets of Los Angeles, into restaurants, asking who was Jewish. Those that admitted it were then beaten. My wife turned to me and said, "Jeremiah 16:16 is here in 2021." What a clear way to show the manifestation of the scripture in Jeremiah.

You will find most Jewish people are hesitant to wear their stars of David or their Yarmulkes (kippahs) out in public today. They have been warned that it is best not to expose their Jewishness.

We also know, through recent history, that when antisemitism and/or economic crises arise, many Jews escape and come back home to Israel. Just as when I came back home from Japan reluctantly, broken and humbled. That is when I recognized my Jewish Messiah, Yeshua. He used the hardships in my life to direct me home to meet Him. If my life in Japan had not become difficult, then I would probably still be in Japan.

The Lord sometimes deals with His people in ways that most Christians cannot comprehend. It seems harsh, but the God of Abraham, Isaac, and Jacob loves His people and has a great plan for their salvation. And unfortunately, it is when we are crushed or against the wall, as we say in today's terms, that the best of us comes out, like olives being crushed to bring forth the olive oil.

So, to all the Messianic rabbis across the world and especially in the West (America), it is your responsibility to tell your congregation to get their papers in order and make plans to come home instead of being hidden in a closet when the hunters come. The responsibility lies in your words of warning and your actions to lead your congregation home. The prophets have spoken, and we must look back, listen, and be obedient.

So as a Jew who was born in Jerusalem, raised in Israel, and served as an IDF tank commander, do I have any right to ask these questions of my own people and to seek the Lord on these answers to "Why the Holocaust?"

I can simply say that the Holocaust had occurred because many Jews did not fear God and have not feared God since the time of Jeremiah. They were focused on themselves, on sacrifices, on tradition. Then after the

107

destruction of the second temple, they focused on the verbal law more than on Him.

Because the Jews, historically, have not feared God, when Yeshua came to the earth, they did not consider that maybe He really was the Son of God. For if they had feared God, they would have never taken the risk of bringing Him to the Romans to be crucified.

And if the 6 million Jews who died in the Holocaust had died fighting in a war and not as the result of being rounded up and sent to concentration camps to die just because they were Jews, then my people would not have understood that it was time to come back home to Israel to build a country and create an army so that a Holocaust would not happen again.

History must not repeat itself! We must heed the words and warnings of the Prophets of old and come home. And just as Jabotinsky said before the Holocaust, "It is time to come home."

I pray that whoever reads this book, believer and non-believer, will benefit from this book, and that if you are a Jew living in exile, you will choose to come home to Israel now. Do not wait until life becomes unbearable or until the hunters come for you. And may you, in turn, be a voice of one calling from the Covenant Land to your relatives and loved ones to also come home. In Yeshua's name I pray. Amen.

But I also know that for the Jews to come back to Israel, they need to know God's love, and so my last chapter will focus on that most important and amazing truth!

# Love

At first, you might be surprised to see a chapter about love in a book that is about the Holocaust. But since this book is about the spiritual aspect of the Holocaust, and faith is a crucial factor in it, then we understand why love deserves a chapter in this book. After all, the first commandment is, "Love God with all your heart..." It does not say worship God or know God but love God.

We do need to get to the bottom of the meaning of love, and so we start with the Hebrew word for love, "ahava," and the root is "ahav."

The middle letter is "Hay," which, as I wrote before, represents God, and when we take that letter out, what is left is the word "av," which means "father" in English. Which means that love is the Father in heaven. As it says in 1 John 4:16, "God is love..."

Throughout the Bible we see various types of love between God and His people Israel, beginning in Exodus when the Lord refers to the people of Israel as sons. The Lord instructed Moses, "Say to the children of Israel, 'You are a stiff-necked people.'" (Exodus 33:5).

And we mentioned that in Hebrews 12:7, the relationship of Israel and God is that of a father and son. "If you endure chastening (discipline), God deals with you as with sons; for what son is there whom a father does not chasten?"

In Ezekiel 16, the relationship between the Lord and Israel is that of a husband and wife. "'Yes, I swore an oath to you and entered into a covenant with you, and you became Mine,' says the Lord God." The Lord is described as a husband who is going to take care of His wife even if she abandons Him and goes after other men. He will forgive her and cover her.

God's love for the people of Israel did not change, but the way it is expressed by the prophets in the Bible did. That was because the people of Israel changed.

In Exodus, they were a group of slaves that were set free after 400 years of slavery, later to become a nation with a country and an army. The people of Israel had grown spiritually during that process, and that means their relationship with God changed. The love of God for His people changed in its expression so that Israel would understand His love for them.

Since God is in control, He allowed the Holocaust to happen. The questions that come immediately are why, and what happened to His love for His people Israel?

Because we are spirit, soul, and body beings, the love that we express to others (people and God) and the love we receive from them is colored and defined by these three factors.

For non-believers, the spirit factor is dormant, and the person is only under the control of the soul (mind and emotions) and the body. Therefore, God's love to them is not being perceived or understood properly.

Unfortunately, this sometimes is the case even for people who believe in God, Christians and Jews alike.

I have already elaborated about how tradition and the Jews' walk of faith before the Holocaust were obstacles to understanding God's will and His love. Now I want to elaborate on what inhibits all of us, Jews and non-Jews, from understanding and perceiving God's love on a personal level.

As I mentioned before, the old self is the self that is connected to your past – your life, your habits, your way of expressing yourself – before coming to know God (Ephesians 4:22-24). That old self, as it says in Roman 6:6, "...was crucified with Him, that the body of sin might be done away with, that we should no longer be slaves of sin." Since we are carrying this cross on our back, the old self still sometimes affects our walk.

We all came to faith in different ways, and the parable of the seeds in Matthew 13:18-30 helps us understand why the result of being saved varies from person to person as we go through the struggles of life. I have quoted this scripture several times because it is a key to understanding our walk of faith and we need to really meditate on it. In this parable we see the different struggles that people who hear the word and get saved go through due to the old self.

In the example of the seed that was sown on rocky places, the person gladly accepted the word. But because the old self does not want to be led by the Spirit, when trouble comes, your mind tells you to focus on the trouble so that you will be overwhelmed and forget the word. The old self pushes you, through your feelings and mind, to focus on your well-being instead of the Lord.

It is also true about the seeds which were sown among thorns – the cares of this world and the deceitfulness of riches overwhelm you and the word is choked out.

Physical survival and comfort are what the old self pushes you to focus on and you feel justified in doing so.

The old self wants to be in control of our total being – spirit, soul and body – and it will not relinquish its control easily. That is why the apostle Paul says in 1 Corinthians 15:31, "...I die daily." He is talking about the struggle with the old self, and that through each battle, a part of the old self dies.

I have experienced that many times as I struggle with the old self that causes me to do and say things that are not in the spirit, and it seems to happen most with my beloved wife. It usually manifests in close relationships and under intense circumstances. For me, it is when I am tired. Then my old self takes over more easily as I am not detached from my feelings regarding my body. Meaning, when I am tired physically, I just want to lie down and close off everything around me. When you live alone, you can do it more easily, but not when you are married. My beloved wife is more detached from her body than I am, and even if she is tired, she is able to overcome her feelings and stay in the spirit. She is a great example for me in this area.

We can see how tiredness affects your spiritual walk. Take Elijah, for instance. After the great victory over the prophets of Baal when Jezebel was threatening to kill him, he was exhausted and prayed that he might die. An angel came and ministered to him and strengthened him for the next journey. "Arise and eat, because the journey is too great for you." (1 Kings 19:7). The Lord is ready to help us in our time of need.

The love I have for my beloved wife, and knowing that my focus should be on Yeshua, is what helps me to deny myself, to die to myself again and again until I get to the point that "...it is no longer I who live, but Christ (Yeshua) lives in Me..." (Galatians 2:20). That is the power of love and why it is essential in our walk of faith.

Again, our old self affects how we receive God's love for us. More correctly, it affects how we perceive His love for us.

And regarding how we view the Holocaust, we all – believers and non-believers – struggle with the old self. Our minds and our feelings prevent us from seeing the Lord's hand in it. Feelings of self-pity can consume us, understandably so, because of what the Nazis did to the Jewish people. By the way, there were also many from other countries who assisted the Nazis in the Holocaust.

But we need to go above those feelings in order to understand why the Lord allowed the Holocaust to happen and to understand that the Holocaust shows that the Lord still cares for His people.

The opposite of love is not hatred but indifference. The Jews in Europe in the 1930's saw the countries of Europe as their home, and if it had been up to them, they would have continued living there if it were not for the Holocaust.

But not so with the Lord. He knew it was not their destiny to remain there. The Lord let the Holocaust happen not out of indifference, but out of love and for the Jews to fulfill their calling as the chosen people. "For out of Zion shall go forth the law, and the word of the Lord from Jerusalem." (Isaiah 2:3).

As a loving Father, the Lord's desire is for His people to come back home. "Therefore, behold, the days are coming," says the Lord, "that they shall no longer say, 'As the Lord lives who brought up the children of Israel from the land of Egypt,' but, 'As the Lord lives who brought up and led the descendants of the house of Israel from the north country and from all the countries where I had driven them.' And they shall dwell in their own land." (Jeremiah 23:7-8). "I will bring them back, and they shall dwell in the midst of Jerusalem. They shall be My people and I will be their God, in truth and righteousness." (Zechariah 8:8). And in Ezekiel 36:26, the Lord said, "I will give you a new heart and put a new spirit within you..."

This shows that the Lord is far from being indifferent to His people. The Jews have been indifferent to knowing His will, but His desire has always been to love them and bring them back to their land.

The Lord also says that He will use force to bring them back, as stated in Ezekiel 20:33-36, "As I live, says the Lord God, "surely with a mighty hand, with an outstretched arm, and with fury poured out, I will rule over you. I will bring you out from the peoples and gather you out of the countries where you are scattered, with a mighty hand, with an outstretched arm, and with fury poured out. And I will bring you into the wilderness of the peoples, and there I will plead My case with you face to face. Just as I pleaded My case (entered into judgement) with your fathers in the wilderness of the land of Egypt, so I will plead My case (enter into judgement) with you," says the Lord God.

The Lord repeats twice the issue of taking His people out of the nation in force and anger. Why?

The Jews have had persecution for centuries, and it did cause some Jews to come back home as early as 1889, the first Aliyah. But, still, the majority stayed in Europe, despite everything.

So, no wonder the Lord had to use force to bring them out. And the anger is due to the lack of discernment of my people, their lack of desire to know the Lord's will, and their overriding desire to just focus on themselves, oblivious to Him.

We see also that judgment will come, besides taking them out of their homes, before coming back to Israel. Ezekiel 20:37 elaborates on the judgment, "I will MAKE YOU PASS under the rod, and I will bring you into the bond of the covenant…"

The Lord mentions here the judgment of the Israelites in the desert, which was a death sentence to all people above the age of 20, except for Joshua and Caleb. The reason for that was to make His people understand that this time also was going to be a harsh judgment.

The rebels that are mentioned in Ezekiel would not reach Israel, either. In the next verse, 20:38, we see the result of the judgment. "I will purge the rebels from among you, and those who transgress against Me; I will bring them out of the country where they dwell, but they shall not enter the land of Israel. Then you will know that I am the Lord."

Judgment seems harsh, but if we think about it, the Lord uses it as a tool to perfect the people of Israel's walk of faith. (Again, "Israel" in Hebrew means "straight with God.") Then we realize that His judgment is out of love and caring.

Also, the Lord does not say, "I will judge you," but, "I will enter into judgement (plead My case) with you." This is like a courtroom, where the Lord, the prosecutor, is on one side, and the people of Israel are on the other. The wording here shows that the Lord is not the judge imposing a sentence. He is pleading His case with the people of Israel "face to face," in verse 35.

The fact that the Lord is furious with the people of Israel, as we see in these scriptures in Ezekiel, does not mean that He has ceased to love His people. It shows that they, like all of us, fall short and are in desperate need of a Savior.

We need to understand that judgment is truly God's love in action, and that will bring my people healing from the Holocaust.

# Day out of the Holocaust – October 7, 2023

That day, Saturday, October 7, 2023, Hamas terrorists broke through Israel's border and attacked 22 villages outside of the Gaza Strip. The horror that they inflicted on the people was like that of the Nazis in the Holocaust. That is why I had to add this chapter to the book.

I was shocked to see how the Hamas terrorists came into Israel with such ease, attacking army bases and villages, going from house to house, killing so many people who were asking where the army was, where the border police were? People calling for help for hours from their shelters for the army to come and save them because the terrorists were at their homes.

It was unbelievably frustrating for all the people of Israel to witness the massacre on TV, as those under attack and their loved ones managed to contact the TV news stations asking them to send the army to their villages. We who were not there felt their pain, their cries for help. We were grieved and angry at the army for not coming to help and that the border was so easily penetrated. It was extremely infuriating and frustrating!!!

People lost their confidence in the army and in the border that was supposed to be so sophisticated and practically impossible to breach.

I asked myself where God was in all of this and why He allowed it to happen? We see in the Bible that God is behind every calamity that fell on Israel; there is always a

117

spiritual reason, as well, that the Lord wants us to learn, and for us to change as a result of it. It is important to try to discern what was behind this horrific event.

I quoted this a couple of times earlier in the book, but it needs to be emphasized again: Isaiah 5:12-13 says, "But they do not regard the work of the Lord, nor consider the operation of His hands. Therefore my people have gone into captivity, (exile) because they have no knowledge (without knowing why)."

We see the result of October 7th in Isaiah 5:15. "Each man shall be humbled, and the eyes of the lofty shall be humbled." The army and the leaders of Israel were humbled on that day. We needed to be humbled.

I had said before that what my people had learned from the Holocaust was that we needed a country of our own with borders and an army so that it could never happen again. Therefore, my people had put their trust in the army and in the land that had secure borders. And I believe that is one reason why that horrible day in October happened; to break my people's trust in those two factors and to cry out to the Lord and to realize that it's not enough to have a border and an army. We need the Lord and we need to trust in Him, which is faith, as I wrote in the first chapter.

The only two things we learned from the Holocaust have shown us that we did not learn enough from the Holocaust.

There is a saying that history repeats itself, and we just accept it as a fact without understanding why. Because we did not learn anything spiritually through the Holocaust, it was bound to happen again, as in this case. I personally believed that something like the Holocaust would need to happen again, but even I could not see how that could come about, since we do have the strongest, most sophisticated army in the region, with borders that are kept on guard twenty-four seven. Until Oct 7th.

I mentioned earlier that in the Book of Jeremiah, the Lord emphasizes the fact that He would bring His people from exile to the land that He had promised to their fathers, and that it would be an even greater and more important exodus. "Therefore, behold, the days are coming," says the Lord, "that they shall no longer say, 'As the Lord lives who brought up the children of Israel from the land of Egypt,' but, 'As the Lord lives who brought up and led the descendants of the house of Israel from the north country and from all the countries where I had driven them.' And they shall dwell in their own land." (Jeremiah 23:7-8). He also says this is Jeremiah 16:14-15.

You can see how important it is to the Lord that His people come back to the land that He had given to their ancestors to worship and serve Him.

The Gaza Strip is part of the Land that the Lord had given to His people, but we gave it away for "peace" and removed our people from their villages, such as in the Gush Katif evacuation.

In Joel 3:2, it talks about the Lord judging all the gentiles who fought Israel, saying, "I will also gather all nations, and bring them down to the Valley of Jehoshaphat; and I will enter into judgment with them there on account of My people, My heritage Israel, whom they have scattered among the nations: they have also divided up My land."

You see that the Lord's judgment will come upon anyone who divides His land, including His own people. The

Lord showed us that it does not bring peace when we give away part of the Promised Land that He gave to us. There has not been peace, and we have suffered His judgment for it since 2005. We will only have peace when we get back what we gave away. That is the conclusion that we have all come to understand after October 7th.

We also have come to understand that we can no longer put our trust in other countries, like Egypt in ancient times, and now in countries like America, for example. The Lord destroyed Egypt so that Israel could not look to them for help. "No longer shall it (Egypt) be the confidence of the house of Israel, but will remind them of their iniquity when they turned to follow them. Then they shall know that I am the Lord God." (Ezekiel 29:16).

And there will come a day when even America will no longer support Israel, and my people will realize they must cry out to the Lord for help. "I will lift up my eyes to the hills – from whence comes my help? My help comes from the Lord, who made heaven and earth." (Psalm 121:1-2).

I hope you can now see why the Lord allowed such a day to happen. What took place was horrible and horrific and my tears are mingled with those of the whole country. I felt sick to my stomach as I watched the videos of what had happened, just as I had felt sick to my stomach when I visited the Auschwitz concentration camp a few years ago.

Grieving and mourning have always been a part of my people's journey, but now is the time we need to rise up with our voices as one nation crying out to the Lord, "Save us!!!"

# Final Thoughts

I would like to summarize and clarify this book with the following story from the 13th chapter of Jeremiah. In the beginning of the chapter, the Lord told Jeremiah to buy a linen sash, put it around his waist, but not to put it in water. Then the Lord told him to go to the Euphrates River and hide it in the crevice of a rock. Many days later, the Lord told him to go back there and take the sash out from where he had been commanded to hide it. He did, and found that it was ruined and useless, profitable for nothing.

Then in verse 9, the Lord explained to Jeremiah, "Thus says the Lord: 'In this manner I will ruin the pride of Judah and the great pride of Jerusalem.'" He further explained the reason why He would do that. "For as the sash clings to the waist of a man, so I have caused the whole house of Israel and the whole house of Judah to cling to Me…that they may become My people…" (verse 11).

The Lord will allow disasters to come upon His people in order to break their pride and humble them, so that they will once again cling to Him.

So as the Holocaust happened, as horrific and devastating as it was to my people, it ended with the country of Israel being born in one day. We must remember that God's thoughts and ways are far above ours, and we must trust His ways of allowing things to happen to bring about a result, in this case, Destination Israel! "Am Israel Chai!!"

Made in the USA
Columbia, SC
28 June 2024

37827962R00070